Best regards
& happy days—
Mary MacHartley

A Hand On Their Shoulder

The Special Love Story At Marbridge Ranch

Mary Mae Hartley

EAKIN PRESS
Austin, Texas

FIRST EDITION

Published in the United States of America
By Eakin Press, P.O. Box 23069, Austin, Texas 78735

ISBN 0-89015-675-1

Front cover photo: Stephen Taylor with miniature horse.

This book is dedicated to God, who is creator of all that Marbridge encompasses.

He gave Jim to Ed and Marge Bridges sixty years ago as inspiration for the Marbridge Plan.

We do not know, visibly, just who *God is — but we know* where *He is: at Marbridge Ranch, where His hand is always on our shoulders.*

— The Marbridge Foundation Board of Directors
— Administrators and Staff
— Supporters and Volunteers
— Families of Residents
— The Marbridge Men and Women
— and, of course,
Ed and Marge Bridges

Weeping willow boughs mingle with bright spring flowers over the little fountain on the grounds of the Marbridge House of Abilene.

A restful corner of the cottage grounds at Marbridge's Community Living Center for women in Abilene. Evening meals at the picnic tables is a favorite spot for relaxed dining or for a table game after supper.

Contents

A commercial crop of big, sweet, white onions brings a grin of success to one of the harvesters, Kim Riley.

Millie Tootle, director of nursing at the Villa, admires the progress of two residents, Robert McLaughlin and Fred Perkins, making a "Dilla from the Villa" banner to hang in the hall.

Introduction

This Is A Love Story

"The success story to be told and retold is that the mentally retarded can *succeed."* *

In the crowded ballroom at Boston's fashionable Sheraton Hotel, Ed Bridges sat with eyes sometimes averted, occasionally glancing at his wife, and listening to the accolades . . .

". . . because of Ed and Marge Bridges the mentally retarded have an opportunity to live a better life. The Bridges are special people and well deserving of the 1982 American Association on Mental Deficiency Special Award . . .

". . . have devoted thirty-five years of their lives to such an effort in the establishment of the non-profit Marbridge Foundation for habilitation of those with limited abilities, but educable. With a big, 440-acre working ranch as the training lodestone, and satellite halfway houses in four cities of the Lone Star State, these two people have built a solid milestone along the road which brought hundreds of adult handicapped and their families out of despair . . ."

Ed's thoughts returned to many years ago.

He was so proud of his baby son, Jim, born of the great love between Ed and his beautiful Marge.

But why does little Jim cry so much? But, Doctor, when will Jim learn to raise his head; he is already over a year old?

There were many "buts" in the young couple's life. Each one seemed to increase Ed's and Marge's determination to find a happy, se-

* All quotes below chapter headings are by Ed Bridges unless otherwise identified.

cure place for their very special son who had some delayed maturity problems.

Out of their tears and terrors — and away from psychiatric advice to "send Jim away, forget him and bear other children" — The Bridges became caught up in an all-consuming compulsion. From now on Ed and Marge resolved that their monies, time, and physical strengths would be devoted to coping with Jim and his problems. They wanted him to be happy and to feel his own worth. Somehow they would together find a way to teach him the beauties of life, believing that God wants every life he creates to have a chance to fulfill a purpose. Jim already was a tall, handsome child and full of love and music.

The crowd at the hotel was applauding, then giving a standing ovation . . .

Ed's thoughts returned to his son's young years, now over fifty years ago, when the slow learners were falsely and cruelly associated with the violent, seriously mentally ill.

"We will find something better for Jim," he and Marge vowed.

Through the pages of this book, the reader will learn how this dream came true for not only their Jim, but others like him. Good business management skills were employed and advice and support was sought from friends and professionals.

They set about this life's work with determination and fortitude, thinking only in positive terms, never looking back and never giving up.

Back in the sparkling hotel ballroom, Ed looked out over the admiring crowd.

. . . and he saw again the youthful Jim, walking his dog through the fields or sitting on the porch listening to radio music. He again heard the squeal of delight when retarded Jacob managed his first perfect dive into Marbridge's swimming pool. And he remembered the pride Steve had in the eight blue ribbons he won in the Austin's Men's Garden Club contest for plants he grew in the Marbridge Ranch greenhouses. He was the first handicapped gardener to be invited to join this prestigious club.

Ed also heard again the beautiful songs the members of Marbridge Glee Club sang at Christmas. He was so proud of the first-place award won by the Marbridge swimming team at the Texas Special Olympics, of the "spirit award" captured by Marbridge Boy Scouts at a Jamboree, of the trophy won by Marbridge contestants in the Senior

Games. These were the things of which accolades are made — many of which only he and Marge shared through the years.

"The men try so hard," he thought to himself. Once a reporter quoted Ed as saying that all they need is "a hand on their shoulder." It was true.

". . . a job well done," said the master-of-ceremonies at the hotel. And now Ed and Marge were at the podium, and Ed was thinking:

"This job will never be done, thank God — because there will always be another Jim, and we will always need to have a place for him."

In 1952 when Jim was twenty-six years old, the Bridges purchased an old run-down ranch fifteen miles south of Austin, Texas, and made it livable for Jim, his Collie dog, and a farm couple. Here he would be safe from the non-caring or non-knowing. Here he could live in a serene rural setting with plenty of fresh air, jobs to do and lots of good food. It was to be "home" and a place of dignity and love for Jim. They were convinced that he would be happy if kept busy with wholesome activities. Their dream grew quickly.

By 1988 the run-down farm has been transformed into a first-class facility that is internationally known as an exemplary one in the field of training and rehabilitating mildly retarded youths and adults. It has spread to accommodate over 450 residents — at the Ranch and at three community living centers in Texas.

But the original Marbridge Plan of Ed and Marge has not changed over the years. They try to give each resident individual attention, lead him to the ultimate he can accomplish and get him to reach his potential with a program to keep him busy. More than five hundred have graduated from Marbridge Ranch to halfway houses in communities or to independent living and working since the Plan was conceived thirty-five years ago.

Today the magic Marbridge Ranch has an enclosed, heated swimming pool, a well-equipped gym, two large dorms, a busy workshop, a school, a new administration building, a retirement village for those reaching the quieter years, an all-faiths Chapel of Love and a cluster of fourteen new cottages occupied by those who have acquired enough skills to work in the outside community but need the support of nearby Marbridge Ranch. The latter is called Mabee Village.

At the hotel, Ed winked at Marge, conveying the thought: "We did it, Marge!" Their Plan worked. They discovered that you *can* teach the mildly retarded to become good citizens and good workers, self-supporting, proud and happy.

Back to 1954, the Bridges took all their savings, borrowed more on their good reputation and made the down payment on their first dream for Jim.

At this time, Ed was a successful merchant in Austin, busy with community and church activities. And so was Marge. Before that first year had passed, the couple realized it would be nice to have a few other young men like Jim who needed a start in a new life. Ed and Marge so easily identified with all those parents who grudgingly placed sons and daughters in private schools and in state institutions, with no other alternative, where the residents were given merely baby-sitting services.

The couple set about igniting the Marbridge Plan in a sensible way. They talked it over with understanding friends, sought advice from interested professionals and formed a board of directors.

"The very first member we appointed to the Board was God, for we believed that with Him on their side, nothing was impossible," Ed recalled.

They proved themselves right! The Marbridge Plan they developed is credited as one of the first pioneer concepts and philosophies that has pointed the way to much of the successful habitation work being done with the mentally retarded across the nation today.

In addition to Ed, Marge — and God — other members of the first board included Howard T. Cox, at that time president of the Capital National Bank; Dr. Carlyle Marney, pastor of the First Baptist Church; M. VanWinkle, a chemical engineer; H. M. Totland, manager of the Woolworth Company; and John H. Winters, director of the Texas Department of Public Welfare, all of Austin. In 1988, all were deceased except Cox, who still served on Marbrige Foundation's Board of Directors.

The Plan began gaining publicity and soon was approved by the Austin Council for Retarded Children, where Ed had long been an active member. Eighteen months after its inception, a federal grant came through — and others would follow. The Marbridge Plan zoomed to importance as the first of its kind.

Most specialists in the mental health area still shook their heads and said the mentally retarded could not be taught a skill. At a steady pace, Marbridge Ranch was proving them wrong! Basically, the Plan was designed to provide an alternate situation for parents who found it

Mama Bridges and Ed Bridges at one of the Marbridge hunting leases.

difficult to locate a suitable environment for a son who could not cope with everyday problems because of certain handicaps.

The Marbridge Ranch provides a sanctuary for them — where happiness for the men is the main objective. A wholesome atmosphere as nearly as possible to family life is provided and careful attention is paid to the good health of the residents. The men are carefully screened by a professional committee. The primary criterion of admission is to be retarded. But each man must have the physical capacity to get around, to work, and to keep up with others. Young men who have histories of delinquencies or serious mental illnesses are never accepted. Marbridge is neither a correctional institution nor a mental hospital. It is a training facility for those lacking normal maturation, but who are educable.

At the ranch a school is provided, but academic grades are considered of less importance than acquiring such skills as social adjustment, emotional stability, physical health, personal care and appearance, use of leisure time, practical information, and vocational proficiency.

At Marbridge Ranch, the men receive an excellent vocational rehabilitation and habilitation program, which enables some to fit into a controlled society or semi-controlled environment in holding some type of job. It also teaches them to live, play, and work with others.

Some of the men at the ranch are in one or two-year training programs. Others are in lifetime residence there, eventually going from active workers to the retirement facility. The Bridges and the board have always tried to work with parents to offer their facilities at as low a cost as possible. It began, and remains, a non-profit foundation.

Mrs. B. (or "Mama B") strongly believes that an abundance of love, good food, recreation, and some "social refinements" benefit anybody — and especially her Jim and others like him. Again, she was right! Even now, at age eighty and with crippling arthritis, she oversees every menu at the sprawling, busy ranch, and is active in most programs, working with the volunteers and quietly adding her counseling to problem areas. And she can still sit in a deer blind on a cold morning and shoot, or sit on a sunny dock and fish.

As a matter of fact, due to Ed's and Marge's love of sport, Marbridge Ranch has a Gun Club, and the men are taken hunting at one of two leases during the season. The Foundation also owns a condo on the Gulf Coast where the men can fish and play on the beach. Some residents spend one or two weeks each summer at the Foundation-owned cabin in Ruidoso, N.M., where they hike the trails, go to the horseraces and have a good vacation. Instilled in the minds of the residents is the idea that they "can do whatever they set out to do." Think positive!

They go into the communities, holding their heads high, attending concerts, rodeos, ballgames, churches, dances. They also eagerly and efficiently assist those less fortunate than they, for they have learned to think in terms of abilities rather than limitations. Once a terrible flood in the city of Austin backed up mud and debris into many homes. The Marbridge men worked night and day to help shovel out the mud and get the homes livable again. The Glee Club entertains at nursing homes in the area, and some Marbridge men served on the nearby Manchaca Volunteer Fire Department team. At the ranch a visitor easily acquires a happy attitude, for Jim and the men tend to spread their happiness around. Meanwhile, Ed, now eighty-one years, retains a firm control on the successful operation he and his wife created thirty-five years ago. Except for vacations with Marge and Jim, visits with friends and hunting and fishing trips, Ed works all day in his office at Marbridge.

Most longtime Marbridge supporters attribute the success of the Plan to Ed's remarkable ability for selling. He knows who to contact for help of any kind; he knows how to organize and complete successful fund drives; he knows how to pick administrators, teachers, and staff; he sets a tempo of busy professionalism in management of the Marbridge Foundation. Ed and Marge Bridges know how to talk to people and secure the most from them — whether a resident, a staffer or a donor. No contribution of any sort, no accomplishment of anyone in the Marbridge empire goes unnoticed. Everybody is recognized for his help, no matter how small.

The honor bestowed on the Bridges by the American Association on Mental Retardation at their Boston meeting in 1981, was cherished by the couple as a high point in their lives. However, it was by no means the only high point. There were the joys of seeing the first residents who graduated marching confidently into community living, the dream realized of a chapel of all faiths built on Marbridge Ranch and the new retirement facility for older residents.

The greatest indicators of the Bridges success, however, are not the buildings or the programs or the services that make up the Marbridge Foundation. Rather the real achievements are the incredible differences they have made in the lives of hundreds of mentally retarded adults and their families and the respect and affection they have earned from Marbridge staff, volunteers, and board members.

Ed, Marge, and their staff sometimes laugh about the many humorous things happening throughout the Foundation which make every day pass easier.

Like the Time:

— A houseparent discovered one of the men sneaking out at night, crawling under a fence to visit a young lady on a neighboring farm.

A counselor took one of the eighteen-year-olds to register for the armed services, as required for each male citizen by law. Needless to say he did not qualify for military duty and, indeed, could not read or write. When asked to sign his name on the final papers, he spoke for the first time as he scrawled his name: "Sure, why any son-of-a-bitch can sign his name."

But the tragedies also came to Marbridge and marked indelible sorrow in the hearts of Ed and Marge, as well as the men, parents and staff.

Like:

— The terrible time a train ran over and killed a resident while he was on a hike.

— Or a fateful day in 1980 when a longtime resident simply

disappeared. Expensive, intensive searches failed to determine what happened.

Marge has never been able to discuss things like these, as she is too overcome with sadness. Fortunately, in the thirty-five-year history of Marbridge Foundation, the tragedies are few. Although never forgotten, the dreams fulfilled must prevail, and the hundreds of lives reworked into pleasant, productive lives must remain at the forefront.

Ed says "We only have positive attitudes. The Foundation will survive one hundred years beyond us, at least." He is counting on the executive committee and the board of directors systems he has devised to continue the Marbridge Plan.

Marge says of the continuation of the Plan: "Boy, if it doesn't, I'll haunt it!" Ed continued "We have operated this on faith. We came to realize that in place of Jim being a burden he became a blessing. It showed us through the trials and errors."

If there had been no Jim Bridges there would be no Marbridge.

The couple loves poetry, and quoted recently in Marbridge's quarterly publication (entitled *The Experience)* was the following anonymous writing.

For Friends of the Handicapped

Blessed are you who take the time
To listen to difficult speech.
For you help me to know that
If I persevere
I can be understood.

Blessed are you who never bid
Me to "hurry up"
Or take my tasks from me
And do them for me,
For I often need time rather
Than help.

Blessed are you who stand beside me
As I enter new and untried ventures,
For my failures will be outweighed
By the times I surprise myself and you.

Blessed are you who asked for my help.
For my greatest need is to be needed.

Blessed are you who understand that
It is difficult for me
To put my thoughts into words.

Five members of the Marbridge choir pose in front of a window in the new Chapel of Love. From left are Peter Norton, Jerry Ladner, Larry Hale, Bobby Sheeks, and Warren Todd.

Blessed are you who with a smile,
Encourage me to try once more.

Blessed are you who never remind me
That today I asked the same question twice.

Blessed are you who respect me
And love me just as I am.

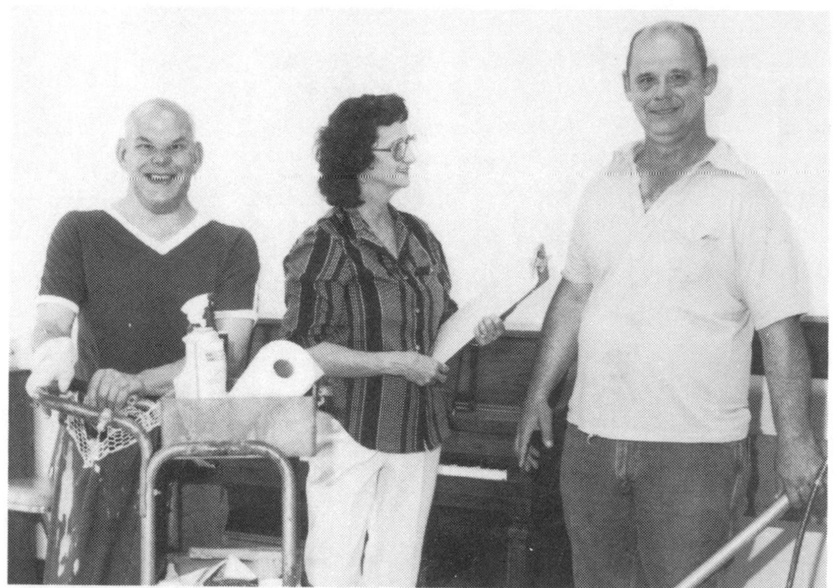

Instruction in housekeeping skills is part of the daily routine for dorm administrator, Betty Douglas. Her pupils, Jody Kahn and Paul Stopford seem more interested in the lady photographer than in the scrubbing details.

Loading up for weekly departure to the bowling alleys in Austin are Walter Robinson, top; Charles McBridge, center and (left to right) in front, Edward Muse, Mark Phillips, and Johnny Adams.

— 1 —

From The Cotton Fields Away

"I learned what a good day's work was at an early age . . ."

Ed was a Christmas present on December 25, 1907, to his parents, Joseph and Molly Bridges, a hard-working and loving couple who brought nine children into the world to keep fed and on the right track toward becoming worthwhile adults. The third of the nine to arrive, Ed had his own special chores on the productive, sixty acre cotton farm located near Inman, Spartanburg County, South Carolina. He advanced from feeding the chickens and slopping the hogs to weeding the vegetable garden and picking cotton.

Ed remembers the hard work after school hours, on Saturday and all summer long — when he worked alongside his sisters and brothers in the fields, orchards, and gardens. All eleven members of the Bridges family worked hard. They had plenty of simple, home-grown food — and very little money, but were happy. Although "King Cotton" was the major money-maker for the Bridges family, the rich Carolina farmland also was very good for producing peaches and apples for the market.

Ed's father used to say, "We have the best peaches in America."

The elder Bridges were active in the small community church. They saw that each of their children became baptised church members.

"My mother was stricter when it came to morals, I think," remembers Ed.

There was the time an older brother and his friend wanted one of the watermelons growing beyond the fence in a neighbor's field. They

The Bridges brought the miniature horses to Marbridge from South Carolina, Mr. B's home state.

told Ed they would give him five cents if he'd go into the patch and bring back a big watermelon. That was a lot of money to tempt Ed! So he did it, not knowing his mother was sitting on their front porch from where she had a fine view of all that went on in that area.

When Ed returned home, the nickel in his pocket, she asked him if he had stolen the neighbor's watermelon. Since he knew he must tell the truth, he admitted the deed. His mother told him to take the nickel and pay the owner for the watermelon — which he did. And which taught him two very good lessons: crime does not pay, and you must pay for what you get.

The Bridges household, always in bustling activity, left no time for sibling fights or much of any controversy from any source. On the other hand, Ed recalls the love and comradeship that prevailed. Especially does he remember the dinner table with its hum of conversation. Years later when he and his wife were searching for a happy place for their son, he was to remember the pleasant home in a rural setting where good food and loving care were in abundance. It was a way of life that was a beginning point for a wholesome career. That was exactly what they needed for son, Jim.

Walking across the cool green fields, swimming in the creeks, picking peaches, eating apples right off the tree, all seemed to help a youth clear his thoughts and appreciate being alive. Years later, Ed was to be thankful that his beginning was in the black soil of a cotton farm.

"My father was inclined to be a little easier on us," says Ed. "He had a good sense of humor and teased us a lot. He used to have nicknames for everything and kept us in good moods most of the time."

However, his father strongly backed his mother in instilling in their children the difference between right and wrong. She pushed Sunday School and always insisted that her children do the right thing — and they remembered it. As Ed advanced into teen years, he began to think that there must be a better way of making a living than in the hot cotton fields. But, of course, he did not complain. In his home, no one complained and no one shirked duties.

He walked less than a mile to Inman to the small town's school. Here he discovered he was good at math, and also made high scores in spelling and English. But he recalls that the town youngsters were prejudiced against the country kids. Rarely were the country kids invited to their parties, for instance. Perhaps this was one of the reasons — which had settled 'way back in his mind — that prompted him to decide when he graduated from high school that he would leave the farm and strike out on his own. Perhaps this also was what caused him to want to own a business. "I always wanted my name on something."

But during these school years, he was a significant contributor to many activities. He entered the declamation contests and discovered that he could speak well and convincingly. The other students listened to him; he could be very persuasive. He had his share of fights; but more often than not, he won his battles by strategy and his wits.

When graduation came for him at Inman, S.C., Ed was selected valedictorian. He asked two friends to listen as he practiced his valedictorian speech, letting his voice reach out across the meadows. He was a handsome and confident young man of almost eighteen. The hills echoed his forceful words, and he felt very eloquent. He was on his way into the great world, and that's what he explained in his farewell address to the school.

"It's going to be a challenge, but we will win it," he told his fellow-students.

So he decided he would go into the world and make his own way. He was going to succeed! He presented a positive attitude which was to prevail in all his endeavors throughout his life. A few days after graduation, young Ed, bronzed from the sun, caught a ride to a nearby site where a dam was being constructed on Lake Lure. He signed on for work. His first job was to take a sledge hammer and manually crush

He may be eighty years of age, but he's still fit and riding at Marbridge Ranch — that's Mr. B at left and David Justin, a ranch resident.

the giant rocks to be used in reinforcing cement. He and a black man worked side by side on the top of the rock pile that seemed unending to both of them. Ed had to keep wiping the sweat from his eyes, and the black man muttered about how hot it was and how hard the rocks were. By noon, the foreman called both to his office and said they just were not doing a good enough job. He gave them their morning's pay and they both left.

Fired from his very first job! Back at the farm, Ed contemplated what to do next. He had always had a restlessness about him — striving to get things done, whether it be homework or farm chores. And he worked long hours until he was convinced he had done his work well. The old restlessness was back, so he went to Hendersonville, North Carolina, where he got a job loading watermelons into a truck for the owner to sell up and down the streets, house to house. Ed slept in the truck at nights. After two weeks of this, he went to the owner's home for a talk, but found that he had left word with his wife that Ed's services would not be needed anymore. A dismissal from his second job!

After thinking about his situation, Ed made the firm decision that he was not, after all, cut out for manual labor, in spite of the fact that he had done such labor all his life up to now on the farm. It soon seemed like a good idea to go to Columbia, S.C., where older brother, Herbert, had a good job in a furniture store. He purchased a train ticket with his earned wages packing watermelons and arrived at his brother's store one day.

"Ed, what in the world are you doing here?" frowned Herbert as he surveyed his younger brother standing there in his old work clothes.

Naturally Ed's appearance embarrassed him, since he was trying very hard to present a sophisticated stance. Herbert took Ed to his home and gave him one of his suits and a good meal and then enrolled him in a business school. They also located a boardinghouse near the school where Ed could live for a small price. This business training was reflected admirably every year of Ed's life, for it enabled him to climb up the success ladder — in his business, as well as in creating and managing Marbridge Ranch.

Soon a small furniture store opened in Columbia and Ed was hired to keep their books on Saturday. Since he was studying bookkeeping in business school, he was good at it. It only took him half a day to maintain the books. So Ed talked the furniture store manager into letting him drive the company truck throughout the city on Saturday afternoon to sell small items, like rocking chairs, linens, flooring, small tables and lamps.

"I sold most of the items for fifty cents down and fifty cents a week, and my commissions kept me in school and in the boardinghouse, so I was able to begin saving a little money." He soon finished his course in bookkeeping, and the store took him on as a full-time salesman. He continued the Saturday pace, however, of keeping the books and selling items from the truck. He also collected the weekly payments for the merchandise. Ed was succeeding! Just like he challenged his graduating class! He was becoming a young business man in Columbia, the capitol city of South Carolina. And he was making money.

His career as a professional in the furniture business was launched. He would climb the ladder, until one day some years later and many states away from South Carolina, Ed would realize one of his lifetime ambitions. But before the fulfillment of this dream, Ed was to experience terrors of nightmares which became real in the daytime. But he would draw strength to fight through the adversities from a partner who loved him.

— 2 —

God Sent Jim

"We thought that he was growing out of his early problems and that he would be a good student after he entered first grade . . ."

Less than a year had passed when eighteen-year-old Ed earned enough money to buy an impressive new red Ford roadster. After all, Columbia was a big city and the Inman country boy, who had already become a good salesman, picked up easily on the correct manners, language and attitude of a city sophisticate — like his older brother.

Columbia, South Carolina, located in one of the original thirteen colonies, sided with the Confederacy in the War between the States. The beautiful city lies between the state's fertile fields on the east, sloping down to a rugged coastline. The lake and mountainous regions lie to the north and west. Lake Murray is empounded by Saluda River to the west. Flowing into Columbia from the northwest is the Broad River, and flowing southwest from the capitol is Congaree River. The Blue Ridges tower on the northwest border.

It was a fun place to be, with plenty of places for picnics and fishing. Ed was confident for such a young businessman, but never overbearing, and he was honest and forthright — traits which enhanced his salesmanship abilities. One night Ed's roommate at the boardinghouse had a date and asked Ed if he would drive them to a carnival that had hit town.

"I'll pay all expenses: gas, refreshments, rides, for all three of us," Ray told Ed.

"O.K.," replied Ed. "Let's go."

Ed had nothing better in mind to do at the time. He was now to enter the portion of his life which, sixty-one years later, he was to classify as the first "high point" in his life. He was to meet his future, lifelong mate.

As soon as Marjorie Davis and Ray climbed into the new roadster, to Ed the world seemed to take on a new light. She was sitting between the boys on the front seat, and perhaps it was the reflection of the Carolina sunset on her golden curls that changed the summer light. The curls perfectly framed Marjorie's pixie face and frolicsome blue eyes. All that evening Ed followed his roommate and date around the amusement park. He didn't have much to say, but he was thinking a lot.

Marge remembers meeting his blue eyes — almost as blue as her own — every time she and Ray went around on the giant ferris wheel or whirled by on some other ride. She also met the same, provocative, yet somehow sincere, eyes staring at her over a ten-cent hot dog and a five-cent cola. Thinking back, Marge said at that time she was impressed with this tall and handsome young man's general aura of youthful strength and purpose.

"He was, and always has been, very gentlemanly," says Mrs. B. "He's also impulsive."

Impulsiveness was proven the next day when Ed walked into her office at the hospital and asked her for a date for the next seven nights. Marge, who was seventeen and one-half years old at the time, was embarrassed and a little upset (but pleased, too). The rules were "no visitors" in the hospital office. But there stood Ed. And, yes, he had a purpose. It was Marge, the girl of his dreams. Thus began a courtship that was as romantic and exciting as any girl could dream, and was concluded some ten months later on December 24, 1926, when Ed and Marge exchanged wedding vows. By this time she was eighteen and the next day he reached age nineteen.

They seemed completely matched, totally in love and ready to support each other, no matter what came, for over sixty years and the romance is still there! Without these commitments, there might never have been a son, Jim, a Marbridge Plan or a successful or enriching life for Ed and Marge Bridges. The wedding was simple but truly lovely, says Marge. It was held at the home of her parents, with friends and families attending.

The young couple spent a weekend honeymoon at a nice, inexpensive hotel in Greenwood, S.C., some fifty miles from Columbia.

Young Ed and Marge Bridges, when their dream was also young.

Marge recalls that she came up with the marriage license fee plus the hotel bill, as Ed was still making sizeable payments on the sporty red Ford roadster. But she didn't mind, and he promised to pay it all back as soon as the car was out of debt. Now, with Marge by his side and a successful salesman's career launched, Ed felt he had the world by its tail.

Although Marge left business school when she married, she continued working at the hospital for several months. Ed fit the mold of the bread-winner and the head of the household, and Marge easily became a satisfied homemaker and filled their first two-room apartment (with bathroom and running water down the hall) with love, laughter, and music. Marge's life had always been focused on music, and she had a beautiful lyric soprano voice.

Marge was born in Old Fort, North Carolina, daughter of W. A. and Mary Ray Davis. Old Fort was located toward the southeast corner of North Carolina; and if she had journeyed over the Blue Ridge Mountains, she would have found that she had been born not seventy miles from Inman, S.C., Ed's hometown. Her father was a real estate executive, mostly handling farm property in nearby Georgia. He played the fiddle and perhaps instilled in his children his own love of music.

Marge was eight when he died. Later her mother remarried and took her family to Columbia, S.C. Marge's new step-father, W. J. Fulbright, was interested in music also. He retained a music teacher to come weekly to their home, and Marge was the one who worked hardest on her vocal talents. Subsequently, she was a choir member, usually a soloist, in every church to which she and Ed belonged. She also was a popular vocalist at many weddings. All of this was pure fun for her, but she practiced hard, and Ed was very proud of her.

Ed continued doing well as a salesman at the furniture store. Some time after the marriage, the store sold out to the well-known Haverty Furniture chain and Ed went along with the deal. Before too long, Ed did so well in sales that his manager gave him a bonus — one of the first electric radios to hit the market. The Atwater Kent machine looked like a simple metal box; but since Marge and Ed had very little entertainment money in those days, it was a lifesaver, especially in the evenings. They heard such artists as W. K. Henderson of Shreveport, Blakely from Del Rio, the Grand Ol' Opry, and Amos and Andy.

About a year and a half after their marriage, Marge announced she was pregnant. They were two excited people, and together the young couple planned a new life around their upcoming parenthood. Days flew by, with Ed working even harder with longer hours to make enough money to save for the baby. Marge's time of deliverance came early one evening, and Ed rushed her to the hospital in his red Ford roadster, now paid for.

In the hospital delivery room, the attendants were reaching a desperation point. Marge was having trouble with a normal delivery. Caesarean sections were only fledgling experiments at that time in medical history, so the country doctor took his forceps and helped bring the baby into the world.

It was a beautiful, 9½-pound boy! A baby son for Marge and Ed! They named him James Edgar Bridges, Jr., and they called him "Jim."

He was a pretty baby, but he kept the couple awake a lot by crying. Marge tried to keep Jim from disturbing Ed, since he worked such long hours at the store. But Jim seemed to cry so much, day and night.

By now, the family had moved into their own house, and Marge spent hours at a time rocking Jim and singing to him. She sang hymns and lullabys in her lovely soprano voice. Undoubtedly that is why, now at almost age sixty, Jim still loves music above most any other entertainment, even radio and television. He collects his own special tapes and has a fine stereo.

When Marge took little Jim to the doctor in his early months, the doctor had no explanation for the crying, or for Jim's susceptibility to colds and other diseases. "Seems like he was always sick," says Mrs. B, and Mr. B adds that "Sometimes we did not know whether Jim would live or not."

Finally, on one of her trips to the doctor, the doctor looked down at the ten-month-old baby — who had yet to hold up his head or turn over by himself — and confirmed something that had already edged its way into Marge's heart: Jim had been brain-damaged in the forced delivery. The Bridges' world was turned upside down! At first the news was unacceptable. Marge cried and sang, cried and rocked. Ed didn't know what to do — but work a little harder and try to comfort her.

Marge would say to her husband: "We *will* teach our son all the things he needs to be happy, because we love him so much and because God sent him to us."

They went to every doctor in Columbia asking questions. Few could offer explanations or solutions. So little was known about brain damage. But the young couple was very determined. Marge and Ed developed an unspoken pact between them that they would never give up on Jim, — that they would find the best way to help him. Perhaps they took to heart one of the mottos of the state of South Carolina: "While I Breathe, I Hope." The other applicable motto of the state was "Prepared in Mind and Resources," which both of the Bridges needed, and had most of their life.

Sometimes in the quiet of the night, Marge would look at her beautiful baby and her heart would become so full of feeling that it seemed she could *will* new energies into her son and he would be all right. She would *will* in her heart so strongly that sometimes she almost became dizzy. Every moment possible she spent with Jim. Everywhere the couple went, they took little Jim along. They were a family.

Soon after Jim was born, the Great Depression of 1929–30 struck the nation. Columbia was an industrial town and many mills shut down; businessmen and stock brokers in New York and Chicago were jumping out of windows; it seemed the country was going down the drain.

Haverty Furniture Company cut back all employees to only four days of work per week. This meant a cut in the salary of one-third of

Ed's wages. However, the manager told his salesmen that if they wanted to get out and work the two other days, calling on customers house-to-house, he would pay commissions.

This suited Ed fine, for with a wife and a sick baby to support, he wanted to make every day count. He hit the sidewalks early mornings and late afternoons on the two days he was off and he made more money per week than before the cut.

When the Depression began to ease, he felt that his manager was not giving him a break in salary, so he joined another chain store in Columbia which paid more commissions plus a straight salary. There was a "method in Ed's madness," however, because there was a rule at Haverty's that made it hard for an employee to be transferred from one store to another in the chain. By leaving the organization and waiting several months, Ed planned to re-apply to his old friend who had been his first manager and who now was managing a Haverty store in Chattanooga, Tennessee. This came about easily, and soon the Bridges family was moving to Chattanooga and Ed was back with Haverty. But they were now much further away from their families than either Ed or Marge had ever been.

The couple began making the rounds of all doctors in that area, trying to find a solution for Jim's learning problems. Although not one would encourage them, the Bridges managed to keep up their spirits, bolstering each other in their unwavering dedication to help Jim. They insisted that somewhere there was an answer.

Chattanooga is located on the Georgia border. The Tennessee River flows into the city, and to the west are the Cumberland Mountains and to the east the Great Smoky Mountains. It has always been a good trade center between Alabama, Georgia, Tennessee, North and South Carolina.

Ed studied the furniture market continuously, worked hard, read a lot about business tactics and became the leading Chattanooga salesman for Haverty, and very near the top for the entire chain. He steadily advanced because of his remarkable salesmanship. Customers trusted him, and he never let them or his employers down.

His performance earned him the position of assistant manager; and as such, he was also in charge of advertising and store display. This was good experience in another phase of selling, and, again, he proved himself capable in this area. But the new duties called for many nights of work, since the advertising and display portions of the business were done after the store closed. Ed explains that "there was not much more money, but more prestige and a very fine chance to learn more about the entire furniture business."

Still the Depression was being felt everywhere; and in addition to his new duties, Ed continued to sell house-to-house. Sometimes he got his prospects on the floor, then went to their homes in the evenings to close the deal. So, on many nights, Marge and little Jim would ride in the Ford coupe, sit in the car and sleep while Ed spent hour after hour selling furniture. He recalls working probably half the nights each week to make enough money to keep his family fed and pay necessary expenses.

Finally, after Jim reached ten months of age, he learned to hold up his head and roll over, and Marge and Ed worked with him to accomplish more and more. At the end of some eighteen months, he was taking his first clumsy steps. He fell a lot. Sometimes they would help him up and sometimes they held back so he could learn to get up for himself. The couple exhibited an almost unmatched patience, and they never gave up. Marge was indefatigable in her efforts to teach Jim to talk. And he did learn to talk, although it was difficult at first to understand him.

Says Marge, "There were the endless, laborious days — day after day — working with Jim, and hoping for Jim."

He grew into a cute and loving preschooler. The couple loved him so much that they knew he would get over his difficult problems and become a normal school student. As always, they thought only in positive thoughts. Marge and Ed prayed together, too, asking God not only for strength for themselves, but for Jim, so that one day he could face life triumphantly.

In Jim's early life, the doctor wanted to keep close watch over him, so Marge had to take him to the doctor three times a week. That amounted to $9 a week, and Ed had to keep working harder than ever.

"The doctor said he had rickets," remembers Mrs. B., so his formula had lots of cod liver oil in it. When he was old enough to eat mashed hard boiled eggs she was told to boil the eggs for one hour. Everything seemed to require more hours than most days had — and more patience than a lot of mothers have. Almost every moment Marge was busy with her young son. She went about it industriously, sometimes with singing, for she knew she must keep trying. She watched every twitch of Jim's muscles, looking for progress in his slow pace of learning basic things. But he *did* make progress. The Bridges were missing Columbia, where they had left so many friends and a church they loved and family, so Ed began quietly working on a transfer to South Carolina. All the road blocks finally gave way, and he was sent back to Haverty's at Columbia as assistant manager to his special friend, Bob Dinkins, who had been his very first manager and who had taught Ed the basics of the retail furniture business.

Ed's long work hours continued, as he had to keep up his sales, be among the leaders on the floor and do other work, too — like advertising and displays. He was now on a straight salary — $50 a week, which was a good salary in those days. Little Jim was now six years old, and it was time to enroll him in the first grade. They had observed that, about some things, Jim had an almost photographic memory.

"He *can* go to school and learn things," insisted Marge.

So dutifully, Marge or Ed took him to school every morning. He did very poorly from the beginning. When Marge picked him up at school, she always quizzed him about the day's activities. Jim would not talk about it, and at times seemed confused. He never wanted to return the next day, and it was hard to make this frightened child continue going to a place that was causing him an obvious fear and unhappiness. But, still, the Bridges thought he would soon get over his first frustrations in a new type of learning-place. Marge had conferences with teachers who, also, were confused and did not know what to do about Jim, as he seemed not to understand most of the work.

Soon, nearly every day Jim came home with rumpled clothes, and Marge suspected that the other children had been picking on him. Sometimes his nose even looked bloody as if he had been hit. She tried in vain to find out what was happening. Was it that Jim did not know how to take care of himself? Could he not learn to play with the others? Again, she knew in her heart that it was true — Jim was not like the other children.

"He's very special," she said, "and needs special treatment. Oh, dear God, who can give my Jim special care?"

Finally, the principal told the Bridges that there was no use in "punishing Jim anymore." He was just not able to keep up with the children his age — he was brain damaged. Of course, thought Marge, when doctors did not fully understand mental retardation, how could teachers and other children? It could have been too discouraging for the Bridges, but to them it was just another set-back and they would go on — for somewhere there would be a happy place for little Jim. Most doctors and teachers did not want to even try to help; most thought the problems unsolvable. Other children and parents were inclined to be a little frightened of Jim.

About this time, the Bridges family returned to Chattanooga for a few years; and Marge and Ed decided against having other children. They decided, instead, to spend their entire life as parents in an effort to help Jim cope with his uncertain life. They always discussed their special concerns with their Baptist pastors, and many times found other parents with similar children with whom they talked. If they heard of a new psychiatrist or counsellor, they went to see the professional.

Marge and Ed were active in church life in their respective communities, and they had many friends. There were parties and trips and programs; they always took Jim along. He cooperated as best he could because he, too, loved people and activity. It was just that sometimes he was confused on details and became bewildered. He needed love and reassurance, which Marge and Ed always gave.

"Oh, he was such a cute little boy," smiles Marge.

Ed was making good money with Haverty's and was well on his way to becoming one of their top managers. Ed says that God has blessed him and Marge with good health all their lives.

"This is one reason we have been able to carry on all these years."

Marge says she has been the worrier of the family and did, indeed, "push" Ed into many activities she thought might be the right one to open needed avenues of help for their son. Ed found himself with unquenched energies which he used in many areas of their various communities. He was the uncontested leader, and Marge was his firm and loving supporter. The second unworded pack between them has always been the habit of discussing together fully every decision that needed to be made. They were good, working partners.

Their road together had already been longer than most couples travel, and Ed and Marge knew there would be more rocky times along the way. But they trusted in God and each other and decided that, somehow, they would also enjoy the scenery along the way. But where and when would their road end? Each day the young couple faced this question. Their youth and courage were in their favor, and they thought positive. Somewhere the road would end, happily for all three in the Bridges family. But they spent fearful, sleepless nights wondering how long will the road be so rocky and, what will be around the next curve?

— 3 —

Beginning Of The Struggle

"There are no set-backs — only disappointments."

Those long, laborous days kept coming — month after month.

Jim could not go to public schools, so Marge spent her days trying to teach him, over and over, and he responded sometimes in a surprising way. He remembered many things, and the Bridges and Jim were happy.

"Sometimes, it seemed like he has a photographic memory," says Marge.

There were times they tried private tutors, but most of them were not really interested in Jim's problems. None were trained to specialize in a child's learning disabilities. So the tutors did not work out. By this time Ed was doing so well that Marge could afford a maid to help with the housework, while she concentrated on Jim.

"We still searched for an appropriate school somewhere," recalls Marge.

And they asked questions of others and sought the advice of pastors and understanding friends. They kept looking for some school that specialized in helping children with limited abilities. They visited schools all over the nation, wrote letters and made phone calls. But most schools turned out to be institutions for merely baby-sitting services.

One day Ed came home with the news that he had heard of a school in Frankfort, Kentucky, called the Stewart School, which might be the one for which they had been searching so long. The couple now lived in Chattanooga, Tennessee, where Ed had been transferred as manager of the big Haverty store. He still worked long hours, but he was making good money and becoming a professional in the lucrative furniture business. When Ed got well entrenched in the store and things running his way, he sat down with Marge to discuss what to do with Jim now.

"Of course," says Ed, "she had been thinking about this all the time."

Since they had found nothing in the Chattanooga area, they decided to visit the Kentucky school. They liked it from the first, so they enrolled Jim who was now nine years old. The Stewart Home School was located on several hundred acres of rolling hills near the Kentucky River. It was founded in 1893 by Dr. John Q. A. Stewart, and the Stewart family still retained control of the special home/school. Quite a bit of emphasis was placed on some academic studies, beginning at the kindergarten level, with a minimum age limit of six years. Older persons, from adulthood, usually were not in the school, but in a portion of the facility designated as "home."

The educational director at the Stewart School was a beautiful young woman named Mary Moore, who seemed to take a special interest in Jim. She was interested in music, like Jim's mother, and she taught him music as well as other things. She was very kind and understanding, and quite intelligent. Perhaps a forerunner of the concept encompassed at Marbridge Ranch, the Stewart School had been dedicated to the belief that some mentally handicapped children could learn. They stressed, also, achieving the fullest development for each child in an environment of love and understanding.

It was over 500 miles round-trip from Chattanooga to Frankfort, but the Bridges drove up almost every other weekend because they missed Jim. Ed and Marge became very fond of Miss Moore and on visits they included her in a lot of the weekend activities. They ate together and sometimes skied in the nearby mountains. It was an enjoyable relationship, and Jim loved it all — Mary, the school, and the weekends of visitation.

Jim was tall and very thin. His father says, "He was awkward and looked like he had not had a square meal in all his life."

But the youngster seemed happy at Stewart School and spent over two years there, with the delightful Miss Moore guiding him. He was learning his ABCs and making progress.

The Bridges, meanwhile, had moved to New Orleans — and that

was a long 1,500 miles from their son in Frankfort, Kentucky. It was almost unbearable to Mrs. B, who now had little demands on her hours in the daytime. She worked in her church, as always, and visited friends, but she longed for little Jim.

Ed was manager of one of the largest, Class A furniture stores in the nation, making an excellent salary and receiving many bonuses for his success in this profession. Marge grew more and more unhappy without Jim, so reluctantly they took him out of the Stewart School and brought him home to New Orleans.

"As silly parents, who perhaps made a great mistake," says Ed, "we had to have him with us — and just when he was gaining self-confidence and making such good progress with Miss Moore."

But now the couple will agree that it was the hand of God, because His plan was not for Jim to remain in Kentucky. There were things to be done. A remarkable turn of events and almost unbelievable coincidence brought Miss Moore back into their lives some sixteen years later.

When Dr. John Peck was signed on as an advisor and consultant in the young years of Marbridge Ranch (1956), he invited Mr. and Mrs. Bridges to his home in west Austin.

— And, lo and behold, there was his wife, their beloved Mary Moore!

What a surprise and what a reunion! Soon Mary, who had always been a fine musician, became Marbridge's first music director. She successfully used music in therapy for the men and was a favorite of the staff and residents.

Mary Moore Peck held a degree in music, but at some point gave up her dream to become a concert pianist in order to marry John Peck and to concentrate on teaching music to the handicapped. (Dr. Peck had been a teacher at the Stewart School where he met Mary.) However, in an unexpected and swift illness (brain hemorrhage) Mary Peck died an untimely death. In her honor the Bridges named a unit of the Foundation's Abilene halfway house. The Abilene house was the first facility founded by Marbridge to accommodate women.

Back in New Orleans, Jim was almost a teen-ager.

"He has made such progress at Stewart School let's try him in public schools now. Perhaps this time everything will be better," said his father.

Within a few days, the principal called the couple to his office and announced that "We cannot accept a mentally retarded student into our school system." The ugly truth came out: the other children

Young Jim Bridges with father Ed in the early days when Ed and Marge were searching for an appropriate school for their son.

and parents were afraid of people like Jim; afraid he might try to molest or mistreat the girls or female teachers. He suggested they have Jim tested by Dr. Ted Waters, one of the top psychiatrists of Tulane Medical School — which they did.

Dr. Waters spent two days in the testing, and called in a psychologist for additional diagnosis. Their advice was: put Jim in some institution, forget him and have other children. These were fighting words to Ed and Marge Bridges! And it was a cruel verdict from the medical profession, and two doctors "who knew nothing whatsoever about mental retardation," says Ed.

They had already determined to spend their lives in an attempt to encourage their Jim to live as normal a life as possible. He already had shown at Stewart School that he *did* have learning capabilities.

All he needed was a chance. They were certainly not going to give up now! The Bridges began their routine: going to doctors in the New Orleans area, asking questions, conferring with pastors and friends. Finally, they located a small school for slow learners called the Magnolia School in New Orleans. On the surface and in talking with administrators, it seemed similar to the Stewart School, and Jim would be in the same city with them.

"Everything is not gold that glitters, however," remarks Ed.

"We soon discovered that they had few special programs for Jim and the other students. There was very little of anything there." It was a simple custodial situation. It did not take Jim long to become bored and want to go home. His mother and father took him out of the Magnolia School, another blank wall.

The Bridges had made many friends in New Orleans; and, as always, they were active in the Baptist Church, Marge with her singing and Ed as a deacon. Marge again tried to work with Jim at home, teaching him things and attempting to keep him busy.

When he was about fourteen years old, Ed and Marge left him one night with the housekeeper and attended a dinner party at a neighbor's home. Soon they received a telephone call from the upset maid. Jim was gone! They hurried home and began searching. Everyone helped. Not too far away was the railway station. They found Jim there. He had walked to the station and told the ticket agent that he wanted to go to Hollywood and become a movie star. Marge will cry and tell you, "My, what that man *could* have done! He was so fine looking. All he needed was a little special attention."

The Bridges knew a fine man in their church who was headmaster of the Rugby Military Academy for Boys. They discussed Jim's situation with him, and he was very kind and understanding. He said, "Why don't you try Jim at our academy?"

So they took Jim for an interview and everyone thought that he might do well there and they might be able to help him. For a while Jim was very happy there, as the staff was considerate and tried very hard with him. He learned some military maneuvers, and Marge and Ed were so proud of him.

"He looked so cute in his cap and uniform when we saw him in a parade," remembers Marge.

Of course, he made no progress academically. It wasn't until the end of the second year that the couple heard a familiar speech: They were wasting their time and money at Rugby; he did not fit in the program. He just could not keep up with the other boys. They also learned that sometimes when Jim could not correctly perform all drills, he would be punished. They were back to Square One.

It was in the busy, colorful coastal city of New Orleans that Marge and Ed began their love affair with fishing and hunting. They had friends with boats, and they went fishing everywhere in that part of Louisiana. Sometimes Jim went along; sometimes he stayed at home with his music. There was always a maid or housekeeper in the home with him.

Ed and Marge Bridges decide to move to Austin, Texas.

Thank goodness for the radio, says Marge, as Jim loved to listen to it for hours at a time. It was also in New Orleans that Marge had her initiation into helping Ed at the furniture store. "One Christmas I went down and sold toys." She liked it, and Ed found she was a good businesswoman. This was going to be a big "plus" for the Bridges in the near future.

But there was always the gnawing pain inside these parents — they knew they must do something else for Jim. He *must* lead as full a life as possible. Now he was in his late teens. They had been all over the country, scouting every possible place about which they read or heard. They followed even the smallest clue in their search for a good, special education school.

"Special education" was a word that was being used nowadays, they learned, by some schools who were teaching courses in mental retardation. No place seemed suitable for Jim. There just seemed to be no real program anywhere — only a baby-sitting situation where they fed them well, sang a few songs and tried to keep them happy.

"It is a waste of Jim's life," Marge and Ed agreed.

They prayed a lot, and their friends joined them in prayer. Would God answer soon?

— 4 —

Big Switch To Texas

". . . and she brought forth her firstborn son, and wrapped him in swaddling clothes, and laid him in a manger because there was no room for them in the inn." —*Luke 2:7, The Holy Bible*

The Bridges family of three loved New Orleans, especially because of a number of very close friends. Among them were Shelby and Josephine Collier. Shelby was fulltime education and music director of the First Baptist Church, where Marge was a member of the choir and a soloist, and Ed was general Sunday school superintendent, a deacon, and active in many other activities at the large church. The Bridges and Colliers ate together, visited together, took trips together, prayed together, and shared sorrows and joys.

It was a real blow to Ed and Marge when Shelby told them he had been asked to move to the First Baptist Church in Austin, Texas, as their education and music director. "I feel 'called'," he declared. "I feel the Lord wants me to accept."

Ed was so saddened by this news that he personally offered Shelby a generous monthly subsidy above his church salary if he would but remain in New Orleans. It was hard for the Colliers to stick to their decision, but stick they did. Ed said a number of years later, "Shelby, Josphine and the Lord knew better than I and so they moved to Austin, but here again it was a big break for the Bridges and Jim, although at the time we did not know it. This was to be a part of our destiny — and somehow we were being led by a higher being."

After the Colliers were situated in the capitol city of Texas, the

Bridges visited them as often as they could. Ed and Marge were determined not to lose track of their friends. Meanwhile, in New Orleans Ed was thinking more and more of his life's professional dream: a desire to own his own furniture store. He remembered all his life wanting "my own name on a store."

He and Marge talked a lot about going back to the states of their respective births or to their old home in Chattanooga. Ed investigated all the furniture stores and possible markets with new opportunities. They would spend many weekends driving to cities in ever direction from New Orleans, considering what area would be the most profitable for a new furniture store. Along their diverse routes, a place, also, for Jim was always in their minds. They talked over their dream with their friends in New Orleans, as well as with the Colliers in Texas.

While Ed was considering all the possible opportunities for fulfilling his dream, Marge listened a lot and kept up her determined search for a special school for Jim. She looked through all kinds of magazines, sent off for brochures and literature. One day her eyes caught a small ad in a magazine. It advertised a school that sounded like it might work for Jim — in, of all places, Austin, Texas.

"Ed," she called excitedly. "There is a school in Austin that sounds like it might be what Jim needs."

So they set off for a visit with the Colliers in Austin and an investigation of the Brown Schools which, to this date, are fine facilities in Texas, with a good reputation for assisting many retarded children and adults. The Bridges also were asking questions of the Colliers and others regarding the furniture business in Austin. Ed and Marge made a decision one day when they returned to New Orleans: they were going to enroll Jim in the Brown Schools at Austin. And they did. And another piece of their puzzle-dream fit into place. The couple, however, missed Jim constantly, especially Marge who was, as usual, not quite as involved every hour of the day as was her busy husband.

Among their good friends in New Orleans were Bill Campbell, a deacon in the church and was Ed's best hunting and fishing partner, and Dr. Ansel Caine, a medical doctor and also a deacon, with whom Ed spent a lot of time. They knew of his dream to own his own business.

In discussing the possibility of beginning his furniture store, Ed found that both Campbell and Caine encouraged him. Knowing his aptitude for business and his special expertise in furniture store management, they declared they wanted to invest in such a business when he decided on the venture.

It took a year and a half of prayer and discussion — and missing Jim — for the Bridges to pull up their Louisiana stakes and head for Central Texas. Their guardian angel was still on the job. It was by chance that a very important location on Austin's main street at 416 Congress Avenue was available for lease. Exactly what Ed wanted. The former businessman there had wanted a larger location to convert his retail hardware store into a wholesale store.

Ed and Marge loved Austin from the start. State capitol of Texas, this city sometimes known as "the friendly city," was a bustling place which relied for most of its economy on the large University of Texas and on the many governmental offices. In addition, there was a big air force base on the outskirts.

Austin had a somewhat mild climate with rich farm lands to the east and cedar-covered hills to the west. The hills formed a half circle about the city, with the Colorado River moving between city and hills. At times the hills took on a pale purple haze — thus the Lone Star State's capitol city was officially called "the city of the violet crown."

Ed had accumulated enough funds to begin his business on a good financial basis. He had the loans from his two friends and all the money from sale of his stock in the Haverty Furniture Company. Over the previous twelve years, with inflation and natural growth of the store, this stock had at least quadrupled.

He leased the Congress Avenue site, and he and Marge opened the doors of what was to become one of Austin's finest furniture stores for the next twenty years. It was built on honesty, high quality furniture and accessories, and Ed's growing reputation as an active and working citizen of the Central Texas area. Marge began working day and night alongside Ed to put their store on firm ground, and to breathe into it a steady growth pattern. She proved that she was a good businesswoman and soon became visible as a creative home design counselor.

The store succeeded immediately, and Marge and Ed threw themselves into activities of the First Baptist Church, civic activities, and social activities. They felt that now they could rest a moment in their quest for a school for Jim, because they felt Mr. and Mrs. Burt P. Brown were operating a facility as near as possible to what they had wanted for Jim.

But after two or three years at Brown Schools, Jim, now in his early twenties, became restless. It grew into an unhappiness. It was always hard to handle their son's unhappiness. It weighed on both Ed's and Marge's minds, and lay heavily on their hearts. Here they were, so close to Jim, where they could visit often and have him home on many occasions. He began running away from the Brown Schools.

"Why did you leave the school and come home," Marge would ask.

And Jim would reply that he was being mistreated and that "Mr. Brown does not love me."

There was one occasion when he was attacked by an older and bigger boy, which precipitated one of the run-away trips. Sometimes Jim would take a cab to the store, appearing in front of his mother's desk, asking for money to pay the cab.

"I did, of course. It seemed like all through the years I have served as the go-between for Jim and Ed."

What made matters even worse was that Jim was beginning to complain to his parents' friends about his school situation.

"Some wondered why we were so cruel in keeping him in the school instead of at home," remembers Ed.

Finally, they reluctantly brought Jim home to stay. Although the Brown Schools were the best the Bridges had found anywhere in the United States, it still had no special training for persons like Jim, who had a higher I.Q. than most of the other residents. Marge and Ed knew they must try to keep Jim busy, but Marge was becoming indispensible at the store all day long. So Ed gave Jim a broom and put him to work in the store's warehouse. "He was to keep the floor and front sidewalk swept, do little chores for the shipping clerk and, in general make himself useful." He received a little salary, and for two or three months it worked out fine.

But, says Ed, "He soon began to have the one special problem that had always plagued him and would remain one of his greatest frustrations: he loved friends and people and was especially attracted to pretty girls.

"He thinks everyone is his friend," remorses Ed, "but when they reject him, especially girls, he has a deep resentment. He does not understand it and reacts in strange ways. He was bitter and wondered why they would treat him so."

When they hurt his feelings, he reacted — verbally — in a somewhat hateful way. Or, sometimes he just sort of pouted and made everyone feel uncomfortable. There might be some, especially the girls, who would be a little frightened of him. During this time, he was attending young people's meetings at the First Baptist Church, and the same old problems arose. Some of the members began discussing the appropriateness of Jim's being allowed to attend these activities, in view of the fact it might cause bitterness in him, and in others about him.

At these times, Jim's heart was not the only one that ached. It was very difficult for Marge and Ed. They *did* understand others feelings, but since Jim was their own flesh and blood, when he was bitter, they could not help but be terribly affected. Then, too, it was awkward so many times with their friends. It became a deeper agonizing situation. What to do with Jim?

He was not working out at the store and, for about the same reasons, he was not working out at the church, or anywhere. The Bridges had tried and tried to help Jim cope with his frustrations which were, in fact, a natural biological urge with females, but one he was unable to either understand or fulfill physically — or emotionally. His parents told him again and again how to act, especially with his peers, but he always forgot when confronting them. All three had felt hurt before. It was nothing new. But the urgency was increasing as Jim got older.

They said, "We must find a place that is comfortable and inspiring for Jim. He needs a place of love and dignity where he can live his life to the fullest."

So when the people of the Baptist church began to rumble, Ed and Marge began long conferences with a very great and compassionate man of God, Dr. Carlyle Marney, pastor of the First Baptist Church. They also talked with several understanding friends and with at least one human relations specialist who was a deacon at the Baptist Church. For many months, they worked hard through these discussions, trying to ascertain their exact position and explore any possible alternatives as parents of a mildly retarded young man. They had done this before, but once more they sought an alternative.

They were looking through a long, dark tunnel, but somewhere about this time in their quest, a little light sparked at the end of that formidable tunnel.

— 5 —

The Nite-Riders

It had become very clear to Ed Bridges that he must create something on his own for his son.

Ed Bridges enthusiastically admits that one of the greatest single influences in both his life and in the founding of the Marbridge Plan was a gentle, yet forceful, preacher named Dr. Carlyle Marney. Marney, now deceased, was pastor of the First Baptist Church in Austin from 1948 to 1958. During the specific years, 1950–51, when the Bridges finally admitted to themselves that there was no place in the nation for Jim, and when they were struggling to find new answers for the old questions revolving around their beloved son, Pastor Marney became Ed's close advisor and confidant.

Subsequently, this gentle giant served on the founding board at Marbridge, and continued to serve on it for many years — even when he left Austin for a new post in North Carolina. Marney backed Ed's search for a home for Jim with his own understanding, enthusiasm, and optimism. He was a springboard at times for Ed's thoughts; at other times, he was a much needed guide through numerous obstacles.

As coincidental as the Bridges' surprise reunion with Mary Moore Peck after many years, was another coincident that happened a few years after Dr. Marney left Austin. His own nephew, Mark Phillips, entered Marbridge as a resident in 1962. So, then, Dr. Marney often returned for visits, not only with the Bridges and Marbridge residents, but with his own nephew.

The last letter which Dr. Marney wrote to Marge, Ed, and Jim before his death in 1978, said:

> On this beautiful Sunday morning in one of Oregon's grand valleys, it seems unbelievable that thirty years have passed since we met the three of you and many precious others in Austin. At least twenty-seven years ago you began to talk of a new kind of place for people whose future would always be a kind of boyhood or girlhood.
>
> The first thing I caught when you invited Totland, Pollard, John Winters, and me to sit with you was that you were going for really competent professional help from the University (of Texas) community. Secondly, I saw you aimed in a responsible competent personal business direction. Third, that you aimed to keep these concerns church-oriented and to see life as full of experience as possible.
>
> Now, twenty-five years after the opening, I can hardly believe my eyes and ears at what has been done — and I rejoice for the hundreds of young men and women whose lives are vastly different. And, of course, I could never have known then that my own nephew, not yet born, would find a home, too, at Marbridge.
>
> All our regard and respect to you and all the dear lay and professional and parent people who have made Marbridge the only one of its kind.

(Today, Mark Phillips is taking it a little easier at Marbridge — in the Senior Dorm, as he is one of the older men residents.)

When cautious members of the church went to Dr. Marney with their concerns regarding acceptance of the mentally handicapped in services, Dr. Marney sought to dispell their fears, but he also fully sympathized with the Bridges' side of this problem. He knew they wanted their son to know a church and a God. He knew that somewhere there would be an answer to their prayers — an answer that would be good for Jim and, perhaps help other parents with similar frustrations.

Still, so little was known about mental retardation and what many citizens knew was often only misguided fear. And any type of handicap in those days received severe rejections.

When these concerns came up regarding Jim's problems, then Ed began meeting with Dr. Marney — at which times they both explored any possible new avenue of action, and new recourse that had not already been tried by the Bridges over the past twenty-plus years.

"There just is no place anywhere for Jim" Ed told Marge, who always cried a little, but who always answered, "There *must* be something. We cannot give up. God will direct us."

Marney also had many sessions with Jim. He eased the young

The late Dr. Carlyle Marney, a board member of Marbridge Foundation, speaking at an early-day gathering of residents' parents.

man's thoughts somewhat — for Jim knew Marney was a friend who loved him. He had confidence in Dr. Marney and Jim felt, then, that God also cared for him. Nevertheless, the agonies stretched on — shared by the Bridges, Jim, their friends who understood and their pastor. It was clear to all of them that Jim and ones like him could never fit in an open society. Many a night, after Ed went home from hours at the furniture store and civic endeavors to face the family problem, he would seek Marney for consultation. Many times they drove around in the night, often not returning home until almost dawn.

Ed says that this good friend "had the great ability to agonize with you but let you do most of the talking."

— And sometimes Jim became a night-rider with Marney, also. Somewhere in these years, either in a church office or in a car at night, Ed must have, almost in desperation, said, "Carlyle, why couldn't Jim have grown up like me — on a wholesome farm doing chores with a caring family and knowing each day would bring some sort of satisfaction?"

Marney might have replied, as thoughts began forming in his own mind, "Would that there were some green and growing place like that for Jim and other of God's children."

. . . and somewhere among these by-ways came the seed of an idea. Who really planted it, no one knows for sure. But it began to grow.

Why not a farm for Jim?

Finally, when Marge and Ed decided that if anything was going to be done for their son, they must create the vehicle, the idea exploded. Ed said, "Let's buy a small farm someplace near Austin and try Jim there in hopes that he can enjoy it. Maybe he would feel secure in the solid soil and maybe he could grow to love that life like I did when I was a boy."

The Bridges felt, for the first time since the birth of Jim almost twenty-five years before, a sense of real anticipation, an excitement that they were close to finding the "treasure" they had so diligently sought. It seemed that this might be the one hopeful plan of action — and it brought a relief that completely overshadowed any thoughts of the work, money and effort involved in such a plan. They were filled with renewed vigor.

"We will make it work, Marge," said Ed, and she replied, "I know, because this is what God meant us to do for Jim. I know this is what we have been looking for."

Ed had built a successful, lucrative profession for himself; he had prestigious standing in his church and in the community; he had provided a good income for his family. If all this did not prove that Ed was a man of creative organization, financial abilities, and leadership qualities, then the creation of the Marbridge Plan certainly did.

He had stamina and dignity, and Marney kept inspiring him and helping him to overcome an understandable complex he had exhibited when dealing with "the professionals." Marney convinced him that, with his first-hand knowledge of the mental retardation problems and his natural common sense, he could look professionals in the eye and let them know that *he* had something to give *them* that was better than book-learning.

Ed was stubborn about the course he felt was needed for Jim and those like him. The professionals who said that mildly retarded people could not be taught skills and could not be expected to lead a full life had not had a Jim. Ed and Marge followed their own advice set many years ago: have a positive attitude, and do not give up.

The plan was that Ed was to borrow needed funds to purchase a land site; and if there were no improvements on it, he would build a large enough place for Jim, a farm couple and, hopefully, several other boys like Jim who needed such a haven.

The Bridges proposed that parents, in similar positions, would pay a certain amount of money each month to cover their son's expenses on the farm.

"It will be a sort of co-op," proposed Ed, "entirely non-profit, and governed by a board of directors." By accepting a few other boys, Jim would have companionship with those he knew liked him and accepted him — and he, them.

It was going to be a happy place! Everything else had failed. It was worth a try. Damn the professionals, and full speed ahead!

Another special contribution to Ed's thinking by Dr. Marney was the idea that all are created equal in God's kingdom. Ed and Marge grew up in the "deep South" where segregation was a way of life that few questioned. Ed says Marney's "teachings of 'One Church' intrigued many of us . . . and under Marney's teaching we were led to understand that, indeed, all men are born equal, that there should be no color or ethnic distinctions.

"This, of course, was a little ahead of the thinking of a few Southern Baptist Churches and ministers. Southern Baptists maybe were not ready to accept a great scholar, author, philosopher, humanitarian, and a great man of God like Marney . . . but Marge and I did. We are proud of his thinking."

From the start, the Marbridge Plan also was completely integrated. It took two years of discussion, intense planning and careful organization to launch the Marbridge Plan. The Bridges knew their basic goals for the project: good food, plenty of fresh air, enough recreation, church services, and social instructions.

To help in the planning, the Bridges gathered together a high level panel of strategists, picked from friends who were the very best in their respective fields. They were not only good friends and/or business acquaintances, but they knew the problems and were entirely in sympathy with the Bridges' concerns and hopes.

To help launch the Marbridge Plan were not only their beloved pastor, but there were Dr. Lee Scarbrough, one of Austin's earliest and finest psychiatrists who did not "run with the pack"; John Winters, well known director of the Texas Department of Welfare and a Baptist deacon; H. M. Totland, manager of the Woolworth Store in Austin and a good friend of Ed; Matthew Van Winkler, next-door neighbor, a good businessman and a chemical engineering professor at The University of Texas; Zollie Steakley, a promising young attorney who was to become a Texas Supreme Court Judge; Howard Cox, prominent banker and close friend of the Bridges; J. C. (Curtis) Pollard, a businessman who with his wife were chief hunting, fishing, and traveling partners with Ed and Marge.

They all realized the need for Ed's proposed Plan and were willing to devote their own time, energies and money to it.

Says Cox: "In those days there were only two courses available for the mentally retarded — incarceration in the state hospitals or pay high prices for a place in a country club-type school which offered only custodial services."

The Coxes had no retarded children in their family, but they spent a lot of time with the Bridges and realized there could be another alternative for such mildly retarded persons as young Jim. Cox could see that Jim certainly was able to learn many things. Cox knew what a waste of a life it would be to put Jim somewhere to sit the rest of his life.

In succeeding years, Cox recalls, "we sort of felt our way along," as nothing like the Marbridge Plan had ever been tried. Cox is very proud of its record. He is a senior executive with Texas Commerce Bank in Austin and partly retired.

Being a certified public accountant who has always advised the Bridges in regard to their finances, both business and personal, Cox is a master fund-raiser himself and has proved invaluable to Marbridge.

Although he has retired also from his work with charities, he has not retired from the Marbridge Foundation. Cox remains the only charter member of the first board. He visits Marbridge Ranch often and knows the boys.

At first, he explains, "we never intended it to be permanent," but it worked out that way. Cox set up a Marbridge foundation of his own of contributors from his private friends which remains in effect.

From the first, Cox told the Bridges that there was no way they could handle building expansions except with funds from private foundations. He provided a list of all foundations, and Ed contacted them. "That's the way we have built so many of the buildings and improvements."

It was not uncommon for Cox to bring a friend to dinner at Marbridge who would, usually, become so "sold" on their operation he or she would become permanent committed donors to the Foundation. Cox knew so many of the Texas wealthy who could afford to give regularly.

At the beginning of the Plan, Cox was "the teacher of fund raising."

One of the first enterprises at Marbridge Ranch was raising chickens and selling eggs.

Ed proved to be not only a good student and quick learner, but also a "master" himself.

"We tried to get everything donated," recalls Cox. "We all helped the Bridges as much as possible. I tried to take a lot of the financial load off Ed's shoulders. At first, I tried to help Marbridge just break even."

When asked in 1988 what he thought would be the next "dream" to be fulfilled for the Marbridge Plan, Cox said, "as long as Ed lives he'll think up something" and I'll help him with it." Officially incorporators of the Marbridge Foundation were Mr. and Mrs. Bridges, Totland, Marney, and Winters. All served on the first board, which also included Cox and Van Winkle.

Ed says that a "silent" member of the panel of planners must have been his mother. "We had a deep love for each other," he recalls. "She always believed in me and kept me thinking that I could accomplish something in life. She is the one who taught me to know God . . ."

Every member of the first board was a close friend to the Bridges. They were intelligent people with the ability to envision dreams and help make them come true for the Marbridge Plan. Each had his own special expertise which he enthusiastically donated to the Bridges. Each was a strong adviser and good businessman.

None of these contributors had a retarded son or daughter, but each seemed to have a remarkable understanding and empathy. Ed says he was very lucky to accumulate such great co-organizers whom he could always count on. After setting up guidelines for a ranch home for Jim and some men like him, the first task was to find a proper site for the "farm." It took several months of real estate hunting, but a desirable piece of land turned up just west of Austin in a newly formed township called West Lake Hills. It was mostly residential. The Bridges bought fifteen acres of land and a small building on Camp Craft Road in the area where the rolling hills of Central Texas begin.

Sparsely settled and private, it seemed the perfect site for the farm/ranch concept which the Bridges and their board envisioned. It was in the old Eanes Tract of Travis County.

Jim could find love, peace and dignity, Marge and Ed thought.

They thought wrong!

—6—

Where All the Jims Are Accepted

"We will treat them as gentlemen, and as sons and brothers, and love them as a part of one large family that belongs to Marge and me, and the other staff members."

In the next few weeks, the Bridges and their board were very busy making plans to set up Marbridge farm/ranch haven on Camp Craft Road. Especially Marge and Ed were inspired. Their enthusiasm was spreading to friends and members of the many organizations in which they were active — like the Texas Association for Retarded Children, Chamber of Commerce, and Texas Vocational Rehabilitation Commission. They talked to everyone they could and received many offers of assistance and promises to do volunteer work on the project.

Bulldozers and other machinery began clearing the land to present the farm picture that the Bridges envisioned — a pretty place with hiking trails, shade trees, animals to love and a little stream for fishing and swimming.

"What will we name it?" Ed asked one evening of several friends gathered at the Bridges home for dinner and a planning session.

After a lot of discussion and suggestions, some just for fun, someone hit on the idea that since Marge and Ed were the "parents" of the new dream, it should be named after them. Finally, at some point someone suggested a combination of their names and enter the idea of "Mar" for Marge and "Bridges" as the family name — and call it "Marbridge." It made an instant hit!

Little did the group know that one day Marbridge would be on

Marbridge buses take residents to town for various events and to church. At left are some of the men in front of the new, air conditioned bus. Administrator Randolph Walker, left, and Mr. Bridges, pose in front of one of the first vehicles, called "the Green Hornet."

the tongues of most mental health professionals as a pioneer in successfully educating the mentally retarded. Or that one day Marbridge Ranch would be known internationally as a model facility, the only one of its kind in the world. They had fifteen acres of land with a farm house, a financial debt, a twenty-four-year-old son with maturity problems and a longtime dream about to be launched. Marbridge sounded exciting to them; Marbridge was a new goal; Marbridge would work! Then all of the above exploded.

It was a shock after about forty-five days of planning and working on the new farm on Camp Craft Road when a representative of the West Lake community appeared at Ed's office in the furniture store and handed him a document.

"What is this?" wondered Ed, unfolding the paper.

It was a bomb thrown directly at his Marbridge farm project. Ed couldn't believe what he was reading — a petition signed by about 200 West Lake residents protesting the founding of Marbridge in their area. It was a terrible blow to the Bridges. To this day they retain sad memories of people they thought would be their new neighbors. These persons were trying to sign away their son's place of "love and dignity." The Bridges realized the people were acting out of ignorance, but they also felt they must be extremely uncaring and non-understanding and perhaps a little afraid.

It was supposed that the residents could only see wild men running all over everyone's property, acting violently and scaring the inhabitants.

"They just didn't know," explains Marge. "Education was what was the matter with those people — and others of that time. We had encountered this before, of course, but our plans for Marbridge included close supervision of residents every moment of the day and night."

One of the most difficult things to comprehend was the fact that the man who spearheaded the petition was at that time a school principal. Of all people, an educator! But, adds Mr. B, "One who knew nothing about mental retardation."

In contrast to the West Lake "neighbors" were the neighbors of Marbridge at Manchaca. Three families have sold their land to Marbridge for needed expansion. "They learned what we were doing," says Ed, "and believed in us. They thought we were good neighbors."

Marge took the biting news of the West Lake petition a little better than her husband. "We will find a way. God will show us."

So now the Bridges faced a decision as to what action to take in view of the hostility of the people of West Lake Hills. What should they do? Could they go ahead with plans? Ed sometimes wanted to, as he was a man who did not admit defeat. The couple discussed it long hours with the newly formed board and with others whose advice they respected. Finally Ed went to Judge Charles Betts, a well-known jurist and close friend. Judge Betts told him he was within his legal rights to set up and operate Marbridge on the Eanes Tract. He added, however, that it might be injudicious to go into a community that was hostile. Every window that was broken, every stick that was stolen, everything bad that happened in the area would be blamed on Marbridge residents. He suggested that Ed might want to think about it and look elsewhere for a site because of the unhappiness and unfairness it would bring to the ranch residents themselves, as well as to the Bridges and their employees. Ed knew that Judge Betts was right.

"Here again the Lord was leading us," stated Ed. One of his furniture store employees had a relative living on an 80-acre tract of

Turkey and chicken raising was an important early day work station at Marbridge Ranch.

land at the small community of Manchaca* some twenty-three miles southwest of Austin. The man's wife, who also worked in Austin, wanted to move closer to the city. This couple, the Jennings, liked the Eanes set-up.

So they worked out a trade which, surely, was "heaven-sent."

Ed traded the couple his Eanes sixteen acres with nice buildings for the Manchaca ninety acres with rundown buildings. But it worked out fine.

The deal was made in 1952, but it took a year to make the Manchaca place livable and workable. Some of Ed's store employees donated many hours of work at the ranch; friends helped rewire all of it; others helped with paint, new plumbing, and furnishings.

Many persons and businesses that had heard of the venture stepped up to assist, as most realized that the Bridges were working on short funds to set up a non-profit organization for the benefit of those who seemed to have missed out on benefits most of their lives.

"It was a labor of love," said Ed. "And we found love came from a lot of unexpected places and people."

---

* Manchaca is a Spanish word, pronounced by the English speaking resident's as MAN-SHACK.

So Marbridge Ranch was officially opened on June 1, 1953, with, as Ed put it, "a prayer, a debt, Jim, his dog named Sir Reggie, a farm couple named Hughes, a team of mules, an old wagon, and a plow."

But it was a beginning. And a glorious one full of hope. Dr. Marney presented the dedication address in ceremonies attended by the Bridges, their new board, and numerous friends. The June 1st ceremony has become an annual event, and one of the biggest traditions at Marbridge where events, small and large, are the occasions for celebrations and festivities. The men love special events, but not any more than the Bridges. All of them seize every opportunity to get together with each other and friends to have a party.

It goes with the Marbridge Plan. In his dedicatory speech, Dr. Marney spoke of the longtime dream of such a place as Marbridge Ranch as a home for Jim.

He called their "quest" of many years a "personal urge by Marge and Ed" to go into one of the "most neglected areas in human relations and most neglected in Christian service . . . people tend to handle problems of their own" leaving no time for others.

He said he knew the Bridges were building a place for many Jims, all of whom "need to belong to their own society" but not knowing where it was. He saluted the couple for "creating a society where these certain kinds of young men can become members" and also for "bringing a new light into a world barely able to understand" this critical segment of the population.

Dr. Marney predicted that "Marbridge will not only be a special society, it will be a home — with a chance to grow and to become happy and fulfilled."

Prior to the Marbridge creation, he said it was, sadly, "only the rich who could afford some special opportunities" for the handicapped, but the non-profit Marbridge "will offer this chance to those that otherwise could not have afforded" a place for habilitation.

He expressed hope that he would live to see its fruition. He did.

From this special date on, the Marbridge Plan was to move quickly, but everything that was put into operation was done with careful consideration and consultation and in a first-class manner. Perhaps that is one of the secrets of the Plans's success. And also from this date on, the Bridges were going to realize that their new goal would now be to help other parents who had sons like Jim. Marbridge Ranch is *where all the Jims are accepted.*

Ed thought that most of his past experiences, even from the time he entered grade school, may have been to prepare him for the development of the Marbridge Plan: his background in administration, personal dealings with the mentally retarded, his deep Christian faith that God would guide him, his wholesome upbringing on a farm and the loyal support of his lifetime partner, Marge.

The farm house sat on one of the highest points in the Manchaca area, overlooking low hills and green grass. The oak trees grew massive, and the woods harbored raccoons, o'possums, rabbits, a colorful variety of birds, bugs, squirrels, and other living things to watch and wonder about. A clear stream of water, known as Bear Creek, flowed freely and at one point gurgled itself into a pretty waterfall.

Actually, there was no real plan at the very start other than this: to give Jim and a few young men a garden to hoe, a cow to milk, hikes and swims to take, good food to eat and recreation to bring fun. There would be occasional trips to town for movies and shopping. It would be a laid-back life which they needed, free from fear, boredom and frustrations. "To be busy" was the key.

Meanwhile, the first year the Bridges were on twenty-four-hour call. Many times Ed or Marge had to "run" from the furniture store to take care of a problem at the ranch. They spent several nights a week on the ranch, and most weekends, to guide Jim and the others.

From the first, Ed as chairman of the board was in firm control. He and Marge knew what Jim needed; they knew what things had been lacking in his life. They worked hard to make up for this past situation. Ed says they spent as much time at the ranch as at their home in town. At first it was hard for Jim to accept moving to the country. He had always been a city boy and had real concerns over the change.

Finally, two things helped him become reconciled to the idea. He had always wanted a dog, but could not have one in the city, so he was promised a puppy; and, Dr. Marney came through loud and clear, as usual, and convinced Jim that moving there would be the best thing. Since Jim loved and trusted his pastor, he felt reassured and agreed to give it a try.

According to plans, the Marbridge ranch house was remodeled to accommodate the farm couple and six boys — Jim and five yet to come. The Bridges wanted the room ready at the beginning, so that they could begin helping other Jims.

They thought six boys would be an adequate number for the project. Jim was alone for six months before five others came along, one by one. It took a year for Jim to become entirely comfortable at the ranch home.

I just didn't know how it would work out," he says now.

In addition to long walks and listening to his radio, Jim remembers that two of his first chores were to water the hogs and feed the chickens. Eddie Shaffer of LaMarque was the first boy to join Jim. Eddie was a large boy and cried a lot. But the companionship of Jim and continuous activity and kindness soon convinced Eddie that he really was "wanted and loved," says Mr. B. So he quit crying and "we got his condition stabilized."

Mrs. B had the major job of handling the homesick boys and those who cried a lot. She knew the hand of a mother would help. Many times she would take the unhappy boy in her car and talk to him while she drove around. It usually worked. Eddie soon was helping Jim with the chores.

Said Mr. B., "I remember how brown Jim was from the sun, pulling that ol' hose around to water the orchard — and Eddie following him."

Among the other first residents were David O' Daniel, for whom a wing in the Senior Dorm at the ranch was named. David was the first Marbridge death. While on a supervised hike in 1958 he was run over by a train. Harold Hartung was the third resident. He did very well with job training and social adjustment, and later worked in a grocery store. News of Marbridge began spreading — some by word-of-mouth. Ed was active in the Texas Association of Retarded Children and was made a lifetime member.

He was well known by the University of Texas special education department, as well as prominent in business organizations and church groups. Soon Marbridge Ranch would be nationally known.

Ed was making speeches over the state, getting letters from over the nation and finding the ranch desperately short on space for acceptable residents. When The University of Texas and a large donor, the Scarbroughs of Austin, became involved, the facility was on its way. A guiding force was Commissioner J. J. Brown of the Texas Vocational Rehabilitation Commission, who found the activities and early successes of the ranch quite interesting. As Ed says, the Commissioner had a "heart of gold." His men visited the ranch, too, and they all liked what they saw.

Two years after Marbridge was opened, through Brown's influence, the ranch received its first grant from the U.S. Health, Education and Welfare department. With this, and being matched two to one by fund drives of the Foundation, they were able to build a dormitory for fourteen men and a larger kitchen.

Previous to this, the Bridges had been pouring a lot of their own money into the non-profit corporation. The first year was particularly financially stressful. They were all hoping the ranch would soon become self-supporting.

Jim is as proud of Marbridge and its success as are his parents. After all, he was its first satisfied resident and its real reason for being. As his parents often say, if it had not been for Jim, there would be no Marbridge.

Jim has an exceptional memory for names, dates and other details. He keeps up with everything that is going on at Marbridge so that, he says, "I won't be surprised at what happens."

At age sixty and a resident now of the Senior Dorm, he is as gentlemanly as his father. He admonishes all residents to "act like a Marbridge Man" always.

He is understandably in a difficult position at the ranch, with his father as manager, president, and board chairman.

"I have no more privileges than the others," he says, although some accuse him of this.

Jim describes his position as an "uphill battle" to keep the men from thinking he's "bossy." Favorite pastimes of Jim are music, humorous TV shows, traveling with his parents, flying and backing all UT Longhorn sports. Although he watches all football and basketball he can on television, he has never wished to play these games. Fast balls scare him a little, he admits, as does swimming, in case someone might push him, and hunting because he just doesn't like guns.

He fondly remembers Marbridge trips — like to Disneyland, the Ice Capades and sunrise services at the ranch's own Todd Amphitheater. He attends Woodlawn Baptist Church with his parents on Sunday mornings, then with most of the Marbridge men he participates in the interdenominational spiritual devotions each Sunday afternoon in the beautiful little Chapel of Love on the ranch campus.

The chapel, completed in May of 1985, had been a special dream for years of Mrs. B, and the longtime Marbridge staffer and Ed's first director, Randolph Walker.

Says Jim, "Randolph Walker built the Chapel of Love, you know." He was its superintendent and usually does all the schematics for new buildings.

The original Ranch — thirty-five years ago — in the rolling purple hills of Central Texas. Painting by Waldene Rust '73.

Jim highly praises the Marbridge Boy Scout Troop and remembers when it received the "spirit" award at a Boy Scout jamboree. "I learned a lot in Boy Scouts, but when I became forty I decided I should not be a Boy Scout any longer."

Several practices which began at Marbridge in 1953 still remain in effect. One is that all men must write home once each week. In the early days Marge and Ed helped a lot of the men write home — even a small note. Today if a resident cannot write, a housemother or some other staffer will help. Communications with parents is important at Marbridge.

The first tuition for the first boys was $75 per month; today it is slightly over $1,000, with parents assuming expenses for all trips, spending money, etc. Working with the Bridges from the start in keeping every move of the Foundation on the correct legal track was a young attorney from the Bridges' church, Zollie Steakley. Steakley later was a state Supreme Court judge.

Said Ed, "Zollie did an excellent job — and, to this day, the original papers and plan have proven to be very wise and exactly what we needed in the way of a charter and by-laws."

After surviving thirty-five years of operation the foundation remains based on the original stated purpose as conceived by its five founders.

This is to provide a training program for retarded young men and women eighteen years of age and over in a creative and wholesome atmosphere where they can learn to live full, rounded and satisfactory lives for themselves by being productive citizens both at the ranch and elsewhere if they leave.

As stated in an earlier chapter, the founders and the first board did not expect Marbridge Ranch to be permanent. According to Howard Cox, who has been a board member from the beginning, they all thought Jim and the several men who joined him would become trained for a vocation and for living in the outside world. But it was learned that some men could not adjust to the outside world, although they were capable of being educated. They would always need support and guidance.

So the Marbridge program soon expanded into a two-fold objective.

The habilitation program teaches the men to learn by doing, and each is rated on performance and achievement. Under this plan, many are adequately prepared for eventual placement on the outside for employment — and, hopefully, they are socially adjusted and emotionally stable.

The Home Program, which includes more than half of the young men at the ranch are for those who will reside there permanently. With constant training activities, they develop the feeling of responsibility and of belonging to a real working ranch which will be their home from the time they enter — until they go into the Retirement Villa for the remainder of their lives.

It remains the expressed intent of the Marbridge Foundation to make available both of these programs for those who are retarded, pass the requirements for entrance and need this specialized guidance and service. Each resident is made to feel he is important. Strict guidelines for acceptance of the men to Marbridge are applied. All must be able to work and play with others and must have emotional stability. Real life work situations are stressed instead of just busy activity which means little. That is why the Marbridge residents feel they are in control of their own lives with their own responsibilities.

Meanwhile, during the first year of operation Marbridge Ranch brought in its first crop — hegari, which they bailed in the pasture. It wasn't a big crop, but they used old fashioned plowing equipment —

the mules and a wagon — and used a lot of manual labor, and they were proud of it.

The next year, 1954, water became a problem. The one small well was not doing the job. So Ed found the money and the men with know-how to drill the first new well on Marbridge Ranch. Also in 1954 the six men and Hughes converted the cow stable into a woodworking shop and ceramics studio. There were no cows at the ranch at that time. Volunteers also helped with the project, and volunteers came at regular times to teach crafts. They fixed part of this old barn into a small auditorium for programs and parties.

"We thought of everything we could to keep them busy all the time," said Ed.

The men were awkward with tools, but under direction, they helped to build the first chicken house large enough to house 400 caged hens. Jim and the other men were fascinated with the chickens and if one of the group was missing, you could count on his being in the henhouse.

Falling exhausted into bed one night, Ed said, "Marge we're doing it! We have built a place for Jim, and I think he likes it."

Mr. and Mrs. Bridges at new Winters Dorm in 1963.

There was a silence. Finally Marge said, "I wish that water well had been an oil well."

Ed laughed, "Maybe one day we will have a gusher."

How, in the world, could this struggling enterprise, built on love and faith, gain a gusher, thought Ed. Did he really have a "tiger by the tail?"

— 7 —

The Plan Ignites

"We think in terms of abilities rather than limitations."

It was tough! Everyone tried hard! One season turned into another those first two years. The young men learned about chickens, planting hegari, slopping the hogs and getting along with each other.

Mama B, who calls all of the men "Honey," came out and played the piano and sang. (Mr. B calls them "our fine boys.") She hugged the boys who were lonesome and cooked special meals on the weekends. Mr. B handled seemingly hundreds of phone calls and personal visits at the furniture store, answering questions about his new venture. His daily mail was getting on the heavy-side. Yes, it did seem he had a tiger by the tail. What he had wished merely for Jim and a few other boys was taking off *big*.

Instinctively, this was a signal for Mr. B. He loved a challenge and he loved a rip-roaring business aura. He thought long and hard about his next steps. How could he deny the pleas by parents just like he and Marge were a few years before, wondering where next to turn for a solution to their son's problems? The first board of directors worked hard, too, putting in many late nights helping the Bridges as they explained necessities for enlarging their dream. Later that first year, the resident men learned more about construction, as a new recreation room was added. Again, friends and others came forward — with donations: a piano, games, chairs and tables — and many took up hammers and saws themselves.

At the dedication, Dr. Marney had kidded the furniture store

Marbridge Ranch's only windmill, named the Brian Ring Windmill.

owners-founders about how beautifully the old ranch house had been decorated. In reality, the furniture store merchandise was top quality and expensive. Sometimes the Bridges brought out furniture, but most of it was donated. Expensive furnishings was not practical for a ranch.

Indeed, one time one of the men locked himself in a bathroom and would not come out. Hours went by. No one could get him to unlock the door. Finally Mr. B arrived — and persuaded him to come out. A scuffle ensued and Mr. B said in this tussle, they broke the only expensive vase he had purchased up to that date.

"I will never forget that vase," laughs Mr. B, who never, again brought out expensive accessories from the store.

The Bridges have always poured private funds into Marbridge, but especially during those first years. Ed launched his first fund drive in 1955, and his expertise at this job was immediately apparent. He raised enough money to build four more rooms, dormitory style, and a bath onto the original ranch house.

By this time there were six men at the ranch and requests for admission for several others. It was in 1956 that a real breakthrough came for the Marbridge Ranch.

J. J. Brown, director of the Texas Division of Vocational Rehabilitation, liked the Marbridge concept and visited many hours with Ed and Marge. In 1956 he referred his first clients to the ranch.

This meant that because of the referrals and on Brown's influence, the federal government gave Marbridge a $20,000 grant through the HEW program. Meanwhile, the first two big private donors emerged to give a giant boost to the facility's financial side. These were the Scarbrough Foundation of Austin and a Mrs. Hutchins of El Campo, Texas.

In the early years, two Texas governors also helped. Price Daniel and Allan Shivers knew Mr. B, were appreciative of his efforts to habilitate the retarded and supported him as best they could with legislative actions and governmental agency help.

Mr. B, in conjunction with several organizations, such as the Texas Association for Retarded Children, lobbied in the state capitol. They were instrumental, finally, in obtaining legislation which assured every citizen in Texas, including retarded boys and girls, a chance for an education.

A continuous emotional influence on Marbridge was Dr. Marney, whose big shadow was eagerly welcomed by men and staff alike, and whose footprints still remain in Marbridge soil. He cherished seeing the Plan unfold. All the men knew him by sight and clustered about him when he visited. He remained a Marbridge influence even when he moved to North Carolina, and remained an influence even after his death.

The First Baptist Church of Austin and its members also have always been good friends to the Bridges and to their dream. There are two things on which Marbridge residents can always rely. Each will receive personal attention according to his need; and at no time will food be withheld for any reason, such as a punishment. Mrs. B continues to direct menus so that good, well balanced food, will always be available, no matter what!

Meanwhile, in those first years, the problems also grew. The board realized that eight men were too much for one farm couple. Actually, they knew these special men needed special help from persons educated to deal with such problems and needs. Keep the men busy, said Mr. B. Nothing is impossible! Think positive! What can we do with the men now? Ed and Marge were constantly being asked.

Dr. Wolfe at The University of Texas's relatively new special education department, watched the building of Marbridge with interest. He became a friend and ex-officio advisor to Ed. Special education was on its way, and so was Marbridge. The two were bound to come together.

Dr. Wolfe suggested the hiring of a regular consultant for the ranch, preferably a professor of special education. And he had a person in mind. He recently had hired Dr. John Peck on his UT staff, and recommended him for the job. Dr. Peck was introduced to the Bridges — and a new era for Marbridge Ranch began.

Dr. Peck's wife, coincidentally, was the lovely Mary Moore that had befriended Jim and his parents at the Frankfort, Kentucky, school when Jim was a small boy.

Dr. Peck was fascinated by the ranch and brought his students to visit. "You won't find this in textbooks," he said. But, then, Dr. Peck was a down-to-earth educator who also had a loving and compassionate heart. Here he could see that the almost-lost boys of the nation were being given a new lease on life. Dr. Peck, now retired from UT, remains with Marbridge to this day. He was the only trained professional psychologist on the administrative team.

The same year, 1956, the first admissions committee for screening applicants was formed, and Dr. Peck and Mr. B worked together on the requirements and procedures which are still followed by the Foundation on all sites. Each resident must be over eighteen years old and be emotionally stable, medically adjusted, able to work and get along with the other men and women. Each is on a trial basis for three months. When a resident obviously does not meet requirements and will not conform, he is immediately sent home.

Previous to the hiring of Dr. Peck and the formation of the admissions committee, the problems of the unacceptable men sometimes became quite demanding and many times dangerous.

Mr. B says, "we had to play it by ear at the first. We met the parents, looked at the young man; and if he looked fairly good, we accepted him without much thought of his past record, any psychological or other pertinent information. We soon learned this was a mistake. There were times when we had schizophrenics, severely emotionally disturbed men. Many would run away at the drop of a hat, and others who would not carry out instructions under any condition.

These caused many tensions, anxieties and sadness, and a professional was certainly needed at this point in the Plan. Many times the Bridges spent all night looking for a run-away, hoping all the while that no harm would come to him or others. It was at this time that Mr. B thought about the tiger he didn't have by the tail right now. And all he and Marge were trying to do was to help others in their same position.

With the acquisition of Dr. Peck as part-time consultant and with counseling from other professionals, this problem began to be solved. The residents were being screened properly. But the founding couple learned during the hard years that "you cannot be all things to all men." Also experience was teaching them the type of resident acceptable at the ranch. With each experience and each year, Mr. B advanced as a knowledgeable figure in the entire mental health spectrum.

There was nothing like Marbridge Ranch — no other facility from which to gain advice. Common sense played a big part, they found, the men were human beings first, and retarded second.

Then, too, both the Bridges believed that a higher power was guiding them. He remembered a good friend of his back in New Orleans named Ollie Webb who convinced him that a person can succeed as a businessman in high places and also serve the Lord well. Webb was president of the Southern Pacific Railroad at that time. Mr. B was finding his words were true.

Early in Marbridge history, Dr. Darrel Mase, a special education professor at the University of Florida who was well known over the nation, focused on the new and unique progress of Marbridge Ranch down in Central Texas. He began recommending it as a model facility that was succeeding in habilitation of retarded men. Dr. Mase took many trips to Manchaca to see the ranch in action.

The same month Dr. Peck was hired, Mr. B found a young man knee-deep in farming and dairying in the blacklands near Round Rock. He had a degree in government and industrial arts from North Texas State University and was a decorated veteran of World War II. Just after the war he worked as a government inspector at the Convair Aircraft plant in Fort Worth, but since he had grown up in the country and loved the land, he had gone to Round Rock to help his brother on a farm. The idea of Marbridge Ranch appealed to him.

In 1956 Randolph Walker became the ranch's first director, working under Mr. B.

Although Walker is easy-going and good natured, he is definitely a workaholic — "like Mr. B," says Walker. He adds that Mr. B knows what he wants, discusses it and expects a full day's work. "Well, I've worked all my life."

At Marbridge, Walker loves the men, and they love him. They

follow him about the ranch — where he would be doing a wide variety of jobs.

One day Walker might be in overalls fixing the plumbing; the next day at his drawing board doing a schematic for a new dorm; the next day he might be dressed in a suit to attend a convention with the Bridges.

Staffers at Marbridge have always done whatever is necessary to get the job done. Controller/vice-president Bob Williamson right-hand man to Mr. B, can be seen serving soft drinks or passing out hamburger buns at the regular outdoor picnics on the ranch.

Walker is now semi-retired and spends two days each week at the ranch. It is very hard to break with the ranch when you have been there through almost every step taken — as Peck and Walker have.

The work at Marbridge "got in Randolph's blood." Walker certainly has been a part of every development step. He always had good ideas, according to the Marbridge founder, and had a concept of all types of construction. He loved to work with his hands, and he loved the men. Walker usually had an answer for the problem at hand, or he found one quickly.

The plan, as first conceived, made provisions for complete medical care of the residents. The first medical advisory staff, all volunteers, was composed of Dr. William Adamson, psychiatrist; Dr. R. E. Swearingen, surgeon; Dr. T. C. McCormick, attending physician; Dr. J. W. Gossett, dentist; and Dr. Philip Worchel, psychologist.

To tend to needs of the soul, the Rev. Bob Perrin, pastor of the Manchaca Baptist Church, became the first chaplain, conducting Sunday school services every week at the ranch.

Not a year has passed at Marbridge without a construction project. This gives the residents work to do, and creates a continuous learning vehicle. Since the beginning Marbridge followed guidelines set by the U.S. Labor Department and pays every man for work, whether chores or assigned work. So Mr. B can never stay still — or stay "put." So he has never stopped dreaming the next dream. There is no way Marbridge Foundation can ever cease building.

"There's always another Jim for us."

In 1957, with fourteen young men to follow him about the ranch, Walker proceeded to gain approval for buying new electric milking equipment for the old red barn which had been converted into the milking room.

"We had to milk the cows at six in the morning and four in the

Mrs. B (or Mama B) teaches social skills to Marbridge men attending one of the first camping sessions in New Mexico.

afternoon. There was a lot of work involved; and with only the men to help, I could see we needed the electric milkers." And not all the men could handle milking. Some didn't like washing the mud off the cows backs."

Soon a full-time man was hired for the dairy department, and Marbridge began selling to dairy wholesalers. Mr. B wanted the ranch to become self-supporting.

An important addition to the staff in 1957 was Mary Peck, who took on the busy job of music and social director. She organized a choir, which the young men loved. No matter a speech impediment — singing is the "language of the angels." It was good therapy, and the men teased each other about their voices.

Mary was especially proud of the annual Christmas program which the choir presented for parents and guests before leaving the ranch for their Christmas holidays. Rehearsals began in October. Since that time, Marbridge has never been without a choir. They don their robes and give programs for the retirement home at the ranch and other groups.

Mary helped Mama B organize the first volunteer social group, consisting of college girls who drove to the ranch at regular weekly times for a social event. Sometimes they gathered around the piano in the recreation room and sang. Sometimes they did folk dancing and always had refreshments, music, and table-games.

Sometimes it was a little difficult to get the parties underway in the gym, the girls knowing the men were . . . "different." But Mary bridged the gap, getting on the piano with a lively tune. She would suddenly stop and ask, "What are we sitting here for? Girls, get those good-looking boys out on this gym floor and into some square dancing." She played music varying from Wagner to "Boogie-woogie."

At this time, Mrs. B became known as the "Pearl Mesta of Texas." Then and now, she knows how to throw a great party. She set the "mode" for all of the Marbridge operations, the slightest occasion brings a festival. Everyone's birthday is observed in some way; all holidays are made into gala affairs. It's possible that no organization hold more parties than Marbridge.

Also about this time Mrs. B began having less and less to do with the initial admission of the young men. Her husband recalls how hard it had been on her.

"I remember well the sadness and emotion we all had in dealing with other parents. They would leave their son and drive away crying. Of course, Marge would cry with them — always. Yet all of us knew this was the best thing to do."

Both Marge and Ed would remember again all those times they had had to leave Jim.

Ed shakes his head. "It was a scene, over and over!"

But the parents had confidence in Marbridge Ranch. They realized that the founders and operators had a son there also and that they would run the program to benefit Jim and all the others, the best way possible. This instilled a needed support from the parents.

"We always keep good communication with the parents or guardians," says Mr. B. "We operate a three-way plan: staff, parents, residents." This is how weekly letter-writing began, and why a regular bulletin to parents is sent. Every man, whether he writes it himself or not, sends a weekly communication home.

Ed and Marge believe that if you organize parents with a cause, anything can be done. They also know that a facility like Marbridge has to be run by a qualified staff — not absent parents. "We must have certain rules," explains Ed. "You cannot direct a person from his parent's home. It's unfair to all of them. But we do have a little trouble sometimes from those parents who just won't let go."

Although now the vast Marbridge facilities encompass up to 400 men and women, there is seldom a hurt not felt by soft-hearted Marge. In addition to helping plan parties, organize volunteers and answer telephones and endless questions, Marge used to swim with the men — in the early days — in nearby Onion Creek or, on the ranch in Bear Creek.

In those days the Bridges wore a lot of hats, fulfilling needs for Jim and the others at the ranch. Probably in their lifetime, this couple played more games of dominoes and checkers than any living persons. They also helped take the men on outings and shopping and to special events off the ranch campus. It was hard for the founding couple to keep one of Austin's best businesses progressing in the daytime, then hurry to the ranch at night to handle all the problems there and take care of whatever was needed, such as helping the men end a full day with a worthwhile activity. Mr. and Mrs. B's bedtime usually was quite late. Sometimes they literally "put the residents to bed" then drove to their own home in Austin.

"We were blessed with good health," says Ed, "which allowed us to keep going."

But if you ask either Ed or Marge, they will admit that they miss the old days when they thought up anything to keep the men busy and happy. "We had to keep them from just sitting around." And every night Marge and Ed thanked God for leading them to the Marbridge Plan — even if it were a twenty-four hour job for them.

Meanwhile, the Marbridge success story was unfolding. The word was out and spreading. Applications for admittance poured in. Everyone was busy. With the hiring of Peck, part-time professional counsellor and consultant, and Walker, full-time everything-man, the load became a little easier for Ed and Marge.

As Marbridge Ranch grew, it became clear that it was of utmost importance that houseparents spend the night with the men. This would take some strain off the Bridges and give the men a security in the evening hours. Houseparents have always become mother-father figures to the residents.

Among the past much loved and longtime houseparents were Charlie and LaVerne Holden, Gerald and Louise Jennings, Louis and Millie McElroy, all of whom served the ranch over a decade; and Lloyd and Johnnie Gentry, who retired in 1988 as relief houseparents for the Senior Dorm.

The Marbridge Plan has had an unsolicited and somewhat uncanny history of pointing the way or setting an example for other facilities. Perhaps it is because it was the *first* of the innovative attempts at habilitation of the retarded that worked, progressed and remains as a successful and model plan.

Mrs. Charlene Crump is the daughter of LaVerne and the late Charlie Holden. She watched the rewards her parents received as houseparents at Marbridge Ranch, and she saw the tremendous work being done at the ranch with the men.

Like some others, she thought there should be a place for women in similar circumstances. She set out to establish such a learning home in Austin for women. Like the Bridges, she did it!

Her Mary Lee Foundation has become as extensive as the Marbridge Foundation. Today they are working together for a common purpose — habilitation of those less fortunate than normal men and women.

Like Marbridge, this facility now also has co-educational facilities and programs which reach across Texas — and the successes are many. In 1988 the Mary Lee Foundation celebrated its 25th anniversary.

Mrs. Crump said in a recent letter to Marbridge:

"In reading an old clipping from my high school newspaper, I was quoted as saying that I hoped to go into social work, possibly to work in an orphanage when I grew up. A few years later my parents went to work at Marbridge Ranch working with mentally handicapped boys and men. My dream of entering some type of social work took a new direction with Marbridge as my inspiration. The Mary Lee Foundation was founded in 1963 and in the ensuing twenty-five years it has served over 2,000 handicapped children and adults. I have never been too proud to copy success or give credit for its source:

And Marbridge was a strong source of motivation in the starting of the Mary Lee Foundation — and continues to be an inspiration to those of us working with the handicapped."

So the "mom-and-pop" operation came to a close. Marbridge was getting to be a larger foundation, and the Bridges assumed administrative directorship roles. Meanwhile the chicken business loomed as a focus of the ranch. In 1958 the one large chicken house was extended, which allowed for increases in caged layers to about 1,000 hens. The whole procedure of the chicken business was good therapy for the men. Some washed the eggs, others counted them, some boxed them. In addition, the men were very good at feeding the chickens and seeing that

In the early days of Marbridge Ranch, residents swam in nearby Bear Creek. Mama B is pictured with some of the early residents — down at the creek.

they had water. Each felt his own worth in doing a needed job. The Plan was working!

A milestone in 1958! The board approved purchase of some eighty acres across the road from the ranch, giving Marbridge about 160 acres in all at that time. Perhaps the one activity in 1958 which excited the men the most was the construction of an athletic field for softball, football, and other field games.

Few men complained when they had to clear the field site of the large rocks. Then they plowed it and removed the additional uprooted rocks. Grass was planted and carefully nurtured. The field remains as one of the most-used tracts on the ranch.

The tragedy of 1958 came not long after the first Boy Scout troop was formed, and a young volunteer, John Harrison, became scout master. On a hike one afternoon twenty-five-year-old David O'Daniel failed to cross the tracks before an unscheduled freight train ran over him, killing him instantly.

Harrison tried to rescue David, getting his own arm almost severed. He was hospitalized for arm surgery, but spent months being treated for the emotional trauma of the death. David was fear-stricken with the realization of the on-coming train and was too heavy to be lifted. Harrison was later cited for heroism and received an award for his efforts to save David at the risk of his own life.

The Bridges were devastated. They took David's death very hard. Mr. B thought perhaps this accident might be the end of Marbridge, that no parent would trust them again. But most of all his heart was breaking for the family of David.

But David's family assured Mr. B that they did not censure him, the ranch or John Harrison. They declared that Marbridge must go on to serve the needs of other young men like David. And it did.

But neither Ed nor Marge have ever gotten over the tragedy themselves. It left an indelible mark in their hearts. When the gym was built and completed the next year, it was named "The David O'Daniel Building." Also, one wing in the Senior Dorm is called "The David O'Daniel Wing." In addition to construction of the gym in 1958, Marbridge Ranch bought its first bus, an eighteen-passenger Ford.

Also, the exterior of the old ranch house was remodeled and the entrance updated. The first large hay barn and hog pen were built. It seemed the economical thing to do was to raise hay to feed the livestock and a storage place was needed. This brought new activities and busier days. The men could choose their activities or the staff placed them where they could achieve the most.

On the cultural side, Mrs. B, Mary Peck, and women volunteers were teaching the residents social skills and good manners — and taking them to church. Dr. Peck and others of the staff, including some volunteers, instructed them in personal adjustments. Mr. B was concerned with the administrative-financial side of the facility.

With the acquisition of the bus, field trips were easier. The men were taken to almost all University of Texas home football games, as well as to movies, musical programs, picnics, shopping. With the addition of the gym, the men learned about such team sports as basketball and volleyball and began playing other teams in the area.

In the next decade for the Marbridge Foundation — 1959 through 1968 — growth in both residents and physical facilities, as well as a steady nationwide "image" development, were phenomenal.

In 1960 alone, the following highlights are remembered:

— Mr. B was elected a director of the South Central Region, National Association for Retarded Children. He was invited to speak and explain the Marbridge Plan at many meetings over the nation.

— A swimming pool was built when resident Harold Kalman's

family gave $4,000 toward it and Robert Lawless's father, Jim, donated all the steel. This meant that swimming could now be incorporated into the ranch's scheduled programs.

— A new woodwork shop was constructed under the direction of Dan Beaver, a counselor.

— A shower-room was added to the ranch house dormitory.

— Pens and hatcheries were built in order to raise game birds — wild duck, pheasant, quail, and chuckar. The express idea was to sell the birds to sportsmen who would release them on their private hunting leases to build up their game supply. This proved good training for Marbridge men, and the program was offered until 1984 when demand for such game hit a slack period.

— Resident Tom Grist's family donated a larger bus, which was painted a wild green color and was named "The Green Hornet."

Parents have always held a very special place in the progress and achievements of Marbridge. Without the parents, their support and their contributions, perhaps Marbridge would have moved much slower. No matter, the Foundation is keenly aware of the parents and their support and very appreciative of all their efforts.

The year 1960 ended with an exciting project for the men. They spent untold hours gathering rocks, all as nearly the same size as possible, whitewashing them and carefully placing them on a hillside near the ranch entrance. The large rock sign, *Marbridge* remains a landmark.

Another longtime staff member who has been important to Marbridge is Ralph Pfluger, currently a vice-president on the board and administrator of the Retirement Villa. He came on the scene in 1961 as a ranch houseparent. Since his discharge from the army after World War II, Pfluger had been ranching in Central Texas.

Having a wife and five children, he really needed a stable job, so he answered a newspaper advertisement placed by Marbridge and, thus, another key personality came into the ranks.

Through the years the Foundation's philosophy for new staff members has been to "bring them up through the ranks, thereby training them 'The Marbridge Way'." This happened to Pfluger. He worked on late night shifts, was a scout leader, and he and wife, Lois, accompanied the men on field trips and vacation trips. Several members of his family also have served Marbridge. Lois was secretary for a few years; two sons worked as houseparents; and daughter, Ann Bayles, currently is employed by the greenhouse.

Pfluger says that when he signed on at Marbridge, there were thirty-eight residents. "We had beds in every nook." He says he has always loved working with those who were catching on to the training and were close to graduation. But, then, he adds that "you can't put a time table on the training — it takes more time for some of the men."

"I learned by doing, and got interested in the whole program. I enjoy helping them and seeing them grow and become happy."

He served on the admissions committee a number of years. Deciding at first he needed to know more about mental problems, he asked Dr. Peck for some books. He spent some years at a Lutheran College, but not in special education, and really laughs when he remembers that "those books of Dr. Peck were too high-powered for me."

Sometimes the admission procedure was difficult. Parents had been known to send a "blurred copy" of important psychiatric reports in their efforts to gain acceptance of a family member.

Most of the men accepted in the early days began learning to work in the chicken department, usually washing the eggs. Pfluger recalls one new resident, Phil from Oregon, who was not happy at all with washing eggs. He took every one and threw it against the wall.

"We had learned that we had to show our men that when we said 'no' we meant it. Patience and firmness finally converted Phil, and it wasn't too long until he was behaving and happily washing eggs."

Leghorns were the kind of chickens Marbridge usually raised, both for eggs and for meat — and they were purchased as fuzzy, yellow chicks. One year, however, the boys were so surprised. They opened the tops of the boxes of new chicks and could not believe what they saw! Black baby chicks and slightly red baby chicks! What were they? It took a lot of explaining to convince them these kinds of chickens, too, were all right to raise.

Also in 1961, a small Gulf service station was donated by the J. W. & Cornelia R. Scarbrough Foundation. The Gulf Oil Company gave all equipment, such as gas pumps and oil racks. It was installed under the direction of Walker and became another work station for the men, as well as a fueling stop for ranch vehicles. The Scarbroughs were unable to attend dedication services for the station, but several Gulf officials were present. Later the company's official magazine ran pictures and an article on this one-of-a-kind Gulf station.

When a man in training at Marbridge does not work out well in one job, the staff tries him at another — and another — until he finds his special "spot."

At this time even with Winston Hall, a men's dormitory, there was the ever-present lack of space for new men waiting to come to the ranch. So the "apartments" were built that could accommodate eight beds.

A significant move of the Foundation in late 1961, which made news throughout the nation, was the establishment of Marbridge's first halfway house. Marbridge chooses to call them "Community Living Centers." This facility was opened in Houston at 5219 LaBranch Street, where it still remains — although by 1988, Houston Marbridge House, like all the other community living centers, had been rebuilt, renovated, redecorated into a very large and modern, model facility.

The Houston house meant an increase in staff and the availability of openings at the ranch when men developed their skills and graduated. Even with this, the ranch continued to expand. The original dining room in the ranch house was enlarged by adding a room, Dining Room 2, and the first large brick dormitory was begun. It was to be called Winters Dorm, after Commissioner Winters of the Texas Department of Welfare. Contractors were Lawless and Alford, Lawless being the father of ranch resident, Robert.

Walker supervised every new construction. The men learned more and more about building. The new dorm, still housing fifty-one men, was dedicated and a bus shed was built with donated funds.

In 1964 a garage was built near the service station to house other vehicles and for storage. Later it was converted into an upholstery shop.

Marbridge was exploring all types of work for their men to learn. And being a non-profit organization, Mr. B and his board stretched every dollar, and every facility. When a building was no longer useful for its original purpose, it was incorporated into another learning station, sold or used for some purpose. Do anything to keep the men busy! And learning, if possible!

"Growth makes change," says Mr. B, "and there is no way to get around it, even the last bus we purchased was now too small for our crowd of men."

So Marbridge Foundation raised some $7,500 by sponsoring a country music show at the Austin City Auditorium. They promptly bought a new forty-eight-passenger bus. A landmark event was a trip to New Mexico. For the first time, the Boy Scouts of Marbridge were allowed to spend a session at the Philmont Scout Ranch at Cimmaron.

Pfluger remembers serving as one of the counselors on this trip. At first the staff was "scared of us" with twenty-four retarded men. However, when the camping session was concluded, it was the Marbridge troop which was honored by a traditional end-of-camp "buffalo roast." Such dinners usually were used to honor visiting dignitaries. The Marbridge retarded men had performed beautifully; the entire camp came to appreciate them; they deserved the honor.

The Bridges went on many of the trips — and still do sometimes. Of course, they accompanied the men to that first Boy Scout camp. Marge taught the men social skills, and Mr. B taught such things as how to make a campfire. The parents of resident Bud Kirk went along, too.

The next year, 1965 the Foundation purchased a recreation lodge at Ruidoso, New Mexico, paid entirely by the parents of the men. The Pflugers were among the counselors on the first one-week vacation trip for some ten men.

Every summer since 1965, Marbridge residents who wished could spend a week's vacation in the high, cool mountain resort area. At first, the groups hiked about the mountains, explored the forests and fished in the trout-filled rivers. Now, however, they always take some time to attend the horse races at famous Ruidoso Downs. Pfluger recalls the first trip and so do many of the longtime residents. They remember loving to watch the prairie dogs pop up from their holes in the ground. Some of the men thought it great fun to stuff apples in the holes. There were lots of apples because there was an orchard on the Marbridge vacation spot.

George was a six-foot, four-inch resident. He considered himself very "macho." So he and a couple of other men decided the first night they would sleep in bags outside — and really rough it. As soon as they got settled in their sleeping bags and all was quiet, Ralph put a blanket over his head and jumped out at the boys.

Said Ralph laughing: "George never even bothered to get out of his bag. Bag and all, he was first one in the house." There were no outdoor sleepers after this trick.

In turn, the men sometimes reversed the fun, and played tricks on the staff members . . . taking the wheels off Walker's pickup . . . putting cow droppings in Holden's boots, . . . in the old ranch house raiding Mrs. B's special "pantry" where they knew she kept all kinds of goodies, . . . or raiding the watermelon patch, playing touch football or racing in the swimming pool.

As Pfluger says, "It's so great to hear them laughing."

One longtime resident of the ranch must be the busiest worker there — as he claims either to have a part in every single good job that is done on the premises — or to have done it entirely by himself. If a bad thing happens, forget him, as he claims no part of that!

Ralph also recalls the first time the Marbridge group went to White Sands, N.M. Since it was so hot there, they decided to get up early and drive to the tourist attraction to cook breakfast. He said when the sun rose on the sands, it made rainbows over the still, white hills. "We could see tracks of the night animals . . . it was unforgettably beautiful."

Since Ralph has been into most of the Marbridge programs, he loves to see again, from time to time, the men trained at the ranch who are successfully working from one of the community living centers.

"It's always a joyous reacquaintance. We are all so proud of these people . . . who represent what Marbridge is all about. Now we are proud of the way the men and women are working together in the new co-educational facility here in Austin."

What really makes his "blood boil," says Ralph, is when an employer takes advantage of one of the women. One woman worker — "a beautiful girl," recalls Ralph — was raped by a prospective employer. "We filed charges and he's now in prison!"

If there might be one thing more rewarding than seeing a Marbridge man accomplish his ultimate, it's the pride of his parents. "They get over being astounded at what we do at first, and then comes the real appreciation," says Ralph.

Pfluger said he was working on the shop roof one day when a resident came walking down with his father — to "show him Ralph." The father laughed up at the Marbridge staffer and said, "I just came to say 'thanks'."

The most significant step for Mr. and Mrs. B in 1965 — and for the entire Marbridge Plan — was their decision to sell the furniture store and spend all their time at Marbridge Ranch.

"We had to make up our minds either to remain in the furniture business and get out of the Marbridge operation entirely, or vice-versa. When it all boiled down there was not much choice because there was no way for us to give up our first love, Marbridge," stated Mr. B.

It happened like this. Marge had left her desk at the front of Bridges Furniture store and was standing in the door of her husband's office. Her face took on a perplexed — almost shocked — look.

Marbridge gym when it was built in 1959. There are many trees now growing about the gym. The field in the foreground is where softball is played.

"What! Sell our furniture store."

Ed said, "I know it's a shock, but Marge, we cannot handle this large furniture store *and* Marbridge. Both have grown; we are needed full time both places. What would you suggest?"

"I think you are right, it makes sense. We are just too divided every hour of our lives."

"Marge, which would you rather spend your working days in?"

"I don't have to think much about that. Of course, I choose Marbridge. After all we have been through to make it a permanent home for Jim and the other men, how could we leave that?"

The decision was made, together, as usual. So, as usual, the Bridges went resolutely about their plan to sell the lucrative, high standard furniture store in downtown Austin, they had founded twenty years before.

In 1965, the present administration building was constructed, and Mr. B was able to occupy the president's office on a full time basis. In later years the building was expanded. Currently it is a pretty and fitting facility for headquarters of the Marbridge Foundation. There are well equipped, computerized offices for the permanent staff and a large and impressive board room. A visitor is greeted by a round fish pond and fountain and immaculate landscaping.

In the wake of selling the furniture store, after twenty years, and moving into the administration offices, the Bridges purchased a home near the ranch the next year. They restored a lovely country homestead on approximately 100 acres of land. It has been the scene of many fun parties. When the couple retires they plan to deed all to Marbridge.

Two other highlights of 1966 were the donation of a small building for use as a barbershop by the Veterans Administration at San Marcos, and the opening of Marbridge's first community living center for women in Houston. Later, all the Houston women moved to larger, newer accommodations at Abilene, which were bought the next year. The community living center in Dallas opened in 1967.

Also, the first summer camp program for retarded boys, ages 12 to 15 years, began at the ranch. This, like most of Marbridge's programs, was a "first" among mental retardation programs in the nation. It worked well, and the Foundation continued the summer camp until 1987.

Early in 1968 a great sadness came to Marbridge. Mary Peck, who had directed the music and social activities for ten years, died of a brain hemorrhage. The ranch choir served as honorary pallbearers at her funeral.

She would have been glad to have seen the progress the remainder of the year, however, for a new wing was added to Winters Dorm, a miniature golf course was built by the men under Walker's direction and the U.S. Government sent a grant to the Foundation to build a third dining room, with a walk-in freezer and a metal shop with complete equipment.

But the star in the ranch's sky in 1968 was opening of the first greenhouse. The only money-making activity devised by the nonprofit Foundation during its thirty-five-year history, the greenhouse has been the Marbridge activity most visible to the general public.

Meanwhile, 1969 was an interesting year. The greenhouse proved so successful that a second greenhouse was built. The men were very interested in plants and how to grow them. They could see almost daily their work — as it sprouted and blossomed. It was exciting.

About this time there was a lot of publicity about how farmers were raising catfish as a money-crop. So Marbridge directors approved construction of four tanks, which put them into the commercial catfish farming business. It did fairly well for the next five years, but competitive prices caused the ranch to discontinue catfish farming in 1974.

Chris Winslow, administrator at the greenhouses, also was in charge of the catfish operation. He said the main reason they found the catfish farming financially unsound was that the tanks needed to be kept full of water by pumping from the wells, and the ground sucked up so much water, that Marbridge was spending more money on electricity to run the pumps than they obtained by sales.

One special man, Robert Lawless, who died at Marbridge of a heart attack at age forty-nine was more interested in the catfish farms than any other person. Winslow said Robert maintained the banks around the tanks, keeping them mowed and neat. Then he fed the fish twice a day. Robert loved to throw the feed into the water and watch the catfish come to the surface. They flopped their tails and generally made frantic waves in the water.

Robert also turned on the irrigation pumps to fill the tanks, and turned them off. He learned to handle the aerators which gave oxygen to the water. He stayed busy all day long in the catfish farming procedure, as long as it lasted. He was sorry to see this work station discontinued.

The largest single donation during the entire thirty-five years of the Marbridge Foundation came in 1969 when W. G. Gildart, who had no family at all, donated 160 acres of land to the ranch which joined his large farm.

Not only did catfish farming become a new work station for the men in this same year, but a laundry and fire truck put the men into laundry stations and initiated many into the volunteer fireman's organization at Manchaca.

Gregg Ring, who was a member of Marbridge Board of Directors (and still remains on the board), donated the latest of laundry equipment, and the ranch constructed a building for it. Director Ring has given much to the Marbridge Foundation, in addition to his time and support, including the natatorium to enclose the swimming pool.

Excitement came to the ranch when it secured a two- and one-half ton truck, plus a tank from some surplus equipment. Under Walker's direction, the men built a fine firetruck which was based on the ranch, but became a part of the Manchaca Volunteer Fire Department's equipment.

Walker founded this fire department and remains — eighteen years later — its only chief. The ranch men "took" to learning how to fight fires, and toward the end of 1969 the ones who were qualified became "volunteer firefighters" for the Manchaca station.

It seemed that 1969 was brimming over with Marbridge activity. A dormitory for summer campers was built, later to become the woodworking shop. A recreation room between the ranch house and Winters Dorm was constructed, and a two-story house near the Marbridge mobile home park was bought and remodeled for the ranch staff.

With so many "hands" to keep busy at the ranch, it was no wonder that so many activities were introduced and facilities constructed.

Marbridge was literally a "beehive" of busy endeavors. Climaxing the year's progress was the construction of an important irrigation system that remains in use.

It had been a very dry year, and an irrigation system was needed to keep stock watered and the greenhouse plants and the landscaping in good, healthy condition. The ranch borrowed the money to install a good system and it has paid its way and been very good as a training station.

When the Yuletide season came in 1969, everyone breathed a sigh, as the year had moved so fast and furiously.

Keep them busy! Keep them happy! The Marbridge Plan was working — overtime, it seemed. And the Marbridge dream, by the founding couple, was in full bloom.

The ranch was seventeen years old — green and growing. The men there were growing, too. They were learning everything from construction and horse wrangling to dancing and lawn trimming. A visitor entering the sprawling, Central Texas habilitation center saw fields of crops, grassy lawns under great oak trees, immaculate dormitories surrounded by beds of flowers and occasionally grazing cattle or horses. To one side of the long straight entrance drive was the professional-looking, adminstration building. Across the parking lot was a swimming pool gently disturbed by a constant breeze.

Everywhere were healthy greenery, men and pets. The men were working happily and confidently, but they always looked up to smile and wave at visitors. The aura was of busy congeniality. Elsewhere, in 1969, the aura was the same at Marbridge's community living centers in Houston, Dallas, Abilene, and Austin.

Almost 350 retarded and brain-damaged men and women lived and worked under the Marbridge Plan, and Marbridge Foundation's board and staff members throughout Texas were skilled and hard-working. But they all had something special too, compassion and understanding and a very special love for their work and the Marbridge men and women.

Ed and Marge Bridges, founders of this pioneer facility, still spent most of their daily hours working, thinking — and dreaming more dreams — about Marbridge.

They were giving prayers of thanksgiving, also to the Lord for accompanying them down the Marbridge road, step-by-step.

— 8 —

By Leaps and Bounds

"The Marbridge Plan had begun to take hold and there was always a need for more beds."

The Texas sun was finally setting in the west, and spreading its good-night glow over the green fields at Marbridge Ranch. Men residents had slowed their daily work-recreation pace and settled in game rooms or their own rooms for quiet time. In later afternoons in Central Texas, even the breezes hold their restlessness in check. So it was this evening. It was quiet enough to hear an occasional mooing of a cow or clucking of an ol' laying hen.

Suddenly a shot disturbed it all. Another followed it. And another. Everyone knew they came from down at the four catfish tanks — where, evidently, Chris Winslow was out shooting snakes again. Winslow, who now supervises the large greenhouse operation, was director of the catfish farming project.

Some parts of the 440-acre ranch were still untouched and produced, among other wild things, numerous snakes. The moccasins, of course, loved the water and found the catfish ponds good hunting grounds for food. But Winslow kept these hunters fairly well under control. Catfish farming was in full swing as a Marbridge Ranch work and learning stations from 1969 until 1974.

Meanwhile, during the decade of the 1970s, hundreds of young men and women came and went as the ranch and the halfway houses of the Marbridge Foundation opened their doors to them. For these young folks, it was a very personal experience, frequently commencing with homesickness and anxieties. But much more frequently it ended in a blossoming of the spirit, an opening of doors they thought could never be opened to them, an opportunity to become productive citizens — and, most important, a chance to grow in self esteem.

Dr. John Peck, a Foundation director and longtime consultant for Marbridge said, "we who play the role of host, who stay on as the residents come and go are apt to measure the years of the 1970s by different measures — like buildings erected, tracts purchased, programs initiated, staff members gained and lost, annual budgets swollen and strained, depreciation, compliance and agencies' demands, etc."

In addition to his other duties, Dr. Peck was named managing editor of *The Experience,* a quarterly newsletter whose first issue was published in January 1973. Dr. Peck remained as its writer/editor in 1988.

The Experience, strove to cover all Marbridge Foundation activities — with regular columns on the ranch, the Villa, and the community living centers. There was also a column written by Mr. B, "From The Desk of the President," and space for listing all contributors for that quarter.

A story in *The Experience* stated that most evident during the 1970s was the astounding expansion for Marbridge community living centers in Dallas, Houston, Abilene, and Austin.

Until the 1970s these were modest dwellings usually managed by a proprietary husband-and-wife team with few helpers and not many residents. But in this decade everything about the centers grew. There were new additions to established houses, moves to larger and more convenient quarters; and places for many more retarded citizens who were capable of learning skills enough to hold jobs in their communities.

It meant that the Marbridge Plan, devised by Ed and Marge Bridges to meet the needs of their special son, was working! By now Mr. B had that tiger firmly by the tail, and the facility he and his wife envisioned and built, which was the lodestone for new satellite programs, had already gone far beyond their original dream. It meant they were now, not only helping their son, Jim, but hundreds of other "Jims."

Because the Marbridge Plan called for delivery of service at cost, there was never money for capital improvement. Any type of construction or other improvements depended on contributions. There were never funds to pay interest on borrowed money.

A really important building project in the 1970s was the senior dormitory at the ranch for those men reaching an age when a slowing-down process seemed desirable. The forty-bed, four-wing, quite pretty and comfortable dorm was promptly, but unofficially, dubbed "The Marbridge Hilton." Built all on one level, as was every Marbridge construction (for convenience of residents with walking handicaps), the senior dorm was the closest to "plush" that the ranch offered, although all the other Marbridge living accommodations were classified as beyond ordinary facilities. Because it featured a huge and beautiful living room, or reception hall, most parties were held at the senior dorm.

The four wings surrounded a beautiful patio. The men kept the trees and plants green and growing, and saw that the water in an oversized pond, complete with rustic bridge, was kept clean and blue.

Altogether the senior dorm was a fitting way-station to retirement at the new Marbridge Retirement Villa. However, the residents of this dorm were by no means reduced to "lounging." Some of the best softball players could be found here. Enthusiasm for picnics, town trips, bowling, hiking and biking, swimming — everything offered by Marbridge — abounded here. At the senior dorm one found that experience was well appreciated.

Take for instance David Justin, one of the first men to come to the ranch over twenty-five years ago. David was "cowboy" because he always spent most of his days, seven days a week, taking good care of the horses and the dogs. He was the uncontested "king of the cowboys" at Marbridge.

David came by his talents naturally. His folks were founders/owners of the famous Justin western boot company in Fort Worth, and had been active Marbridge supporters over two decades.

The construction of the Richardson Horse Stables was made possible by the Sid Richardson Foundation of Fort Worth in 1977. Donations to the Foundation came in almost daily, some large and some small, but "all very much appreciated." Gregg Ring, father of two Marbridge men, donated the natatorium to allow for year-round use of the swimming pool.

And what is a ranch without a windmill? So Ring also donated a windmill and well in the same decade. It is called the Brian Ring Windmill.

Mr. and Mrs. W. L. Todd, parents of resident, Warren, donated the amphitheater where outdoor meetings, celebrations, songfests and special programs are held in good weather. It adjoins a shaded park where residents have picnics as often as possible. Nothing like Texas fresh air.

Todd Amphitheater also is the annual scene of Easter sunrise services which always draw a crowd.

Beginning the first year of the 1970s, Walker and the men built a low-water crossing at Bear Creek to allow access from the ranch to the newly acquired Gildart property. Bear Creek was used for swimming in the early days, but now continues to be a beautiful place for picnics and hiking. It is one of the chief natural beauty spots on the ranch. Rugged cliffs bank the creek which runs cool and deep between large oaks, tangled greenery and tall grass.

An energetic project of building hike and bike trails kept the men and staff busy for a long time in 1971. When they were completed, the Foundation dug into its pockets and bought new bicycles, including several three-wheelers. Also in this year the new bath house at the swimming pool was built under Walker's direction.

The year 1972 was busy and eventful. No one expected less — for at Marbridge things happened — all the time. No standing still for the dream of Ed and Marge Bridges.

In 1972, a second mobile home was purchased and placed in the mobile home park for staffers at the edge of the ranch, and a complete waste water system, including machinery and sedimentation pools, was installed. A focal point for a work station, a slaughtering and processing plant, was built. Here the men learned how to process chickens, turkeys, and catfish.

Two buses were purchased, an air-conditioned thirty-six-passenger International and a smaller thirty-two-passenger Chevrolet. A relatively new dream of providing a second dorm on the ranch campus for the men who had slowed down a bit and needed more leisure was included when the senior dorm was built and occupied.

Mr. B had been at his best when planning this step — he asked parents of men who would probably want to move to the senior accommodations for donations and also applied for a grant. Both were successful.

A very exciting time came when a four-man swimming team from Marbridge won four medals at the National Special Olympics in Los Angeles. This marked the first national recognition for Marbridge in the field of sports.

On the much applauded team were Bill McLemour, John Queen, Steve Schlueter, and Paul Stopford. The year 1973 opened fittingly in

January with formal dedication of the senior dorm by Dr. Charlyle Marney, a board member and incorporator of the Foundation.

Among other attributes, Dr. Marney had a great sense of humor, and it came through very clearly in his speeches and sermons.

In his dedicatory address at the ranch, he said, "I don't know how Margie (Bridges) can love 400 sons at one time, but she can."

Further, he kidded the Bridges about the furniture in the first little ranch house, indicating they used some of the fine furnishings from their store. "I thought that small house with only a few boys was amazingly well furnished."

Dr. Marney reminded the audience that a new quality of life for the retarded had come from and "branched out from this Central Texas facility. The Bridges and their operation has ministered to many over the years."

Recalling the small beginning, he mentioned how proud he had been to see it grow, and how proud he was that it was totally non-sectarian and non-segregated.

"Margie and Ed have become authorities in the mental health field," he said, "by trial and error . . . at the facility which was the first and most advanced of its kind. Graduate students come to study it . . ."

He told the listeners to "look around and know that your donations have not gone down the drain here. They never will."

The dedication ceremony ended with the traditional hymn sung at most Marbridge ceremonies, "Bless This House."

To accommodate more men, one of the old recreation rooms at Winston Hall (now Winters Dorm) was converted into a dormitory with bunk beds and was divided into bedroom, dayroom, and bathroom.

During this year also, the ranch installed central heating and air conditioning to the ranch house and dining rooms. Pfluger who had been gone from the ranch almost a year returned to the staff and was appointed business manager.

The first of several fires during this decade destroyed the hay barn and some 12,000 bales of hay. So the original chicken house was converted to a hay barn, but the loss of hay represented a severe financial loss to the Foundation ranch program.

While this was going on, Mr. B proved that he and the board had enough know-how to get a deal-worth-getting concluded.

Since Marbridge House, Abilene had been moving so swiftly and many were on the waiting list, the time was ripe to buy larger quar-

Marbridge men with the firetruck, washing the parking lot at the retirement Villa.

ters. A real estate man in that area hinted that old St. Ann's Hospital and grounds could be gotten for much less than the quoted price.

"We worked it all out," said Mr. B, when he learned that the broker handling it was about to let one of his other clients purchase the building.

Mr. B went into action. He visited the Catholic sister in charge who lived in San Antonio. She knew of the Marbridge Foundation and its work. The director at Abilene also had done a lot of leg work behind the scenes — and soon the real estate man found himself outsmarted and the Foundation found they had purchased the desired property. They offered just a slightly higher price than the low offer suggested by the realtor — got the bid — and became new owners of St. Ann's Hospital site.

The Abilene house became perhaps the most complete program of any of the Marbridge houses, It had a co-op house, private apartments for those able to live away from the co-op support and a training rehab wing.

A fine new hay barn was built near Bear Creek in 1974, as well as a slat house for plants in the greenhouse area.

Dedication ceremonies were held for the opening of the new Mary Peck Dormitory at the Abilene facility and also for the completion of the swimming pool building at the ranch, named Ring Natatorium. The latter was held during the Marbridge 21st anniversary party.

Some of the men were sad to see the dairy and catfish farm go. Both were discontinued because of competitive prices in the market place and because of financial reversals in both areas.

At this time the ranch launched into beef cattle, stocking the pasture with quality cows and calves. Pfluger was in charge of the activity and work station.

Shelby Collier, who four years earlier had been the ranch's first horticulture director, (as well as choir director) resigned due to health reasons.

Winslow, now out of the catfish farming business, was named director of all horticulture and the greenhouses. He remained in this position in 1988, having helped to build up this operation as a money-maker.

In 1988 the greenhouses provided a profit and became Marbridge's best link to the public.

Mr. B. said of Collier: "He is one of the best public relations persons and the best advertising men I have ever known — even tho' he has never been in that area professionally."

But before he arrived for work he had already secured a nice donation from a parent in Arkansas and a loan to be used to build the first greenhouse. Specifically, the greenhouse was to be used for growing tomatoes. Tomatoes, it seemed, were considered a good money crop in 1968.

Collier's energy was transferred to the men who were working under him, and they all worked long, hard hours. Everyone was sure the tomato crop would be very profitable.

The first year the greenhouse did fairly well, but with the second year came a hot drought, and, as Mr. B says "We lost our shirts."

Perhaps Collier saw it coming, but he had been busy behind scenes making a complete study of the whole greenhouse profession. He read all he could; he visited many garden clubs; he questioned horticulturists and gardeners.

He was convinced that Marbridge Ranch needed to convert its greenhouse into nursery plants. He believed that a large segment of the population simply could not do without beautiful indoor and outdoor plants, especially hanging plants. He was right. Mr. B was right in accepting his solution.

The succeeding years would see the ranch build ten more greenhouses and fill them with gorgeous, healthy, varied plant selections. It became the one, good money-maker for the non-profit Marbridge Foundation, which always needed more funds. Toward the end of 1974, the Foundation enhanced the fire-fighting equipment on the ranch by purchasing an International cab-over fire truck. This added to the training station in the firefighting department.

Randolph taught the men things that even their parents believed their sons could not do. During all thirty-five years of Marbridge, the challenge had been there, and the drive to succeed emersed. Mr. B and his staff were not miracle workers — just workers who somehow could gently bring out the miracles inside these handicapped men and women.

At the ranch, many of the men had become experts-of-sorts in some field. In 1975, the construction workers gathered about Walker, and they built the fountain at the administration building and a new barber shop. Now the men did not have to be taken off campus to get their haircuts.

Dr. Peck retired from The University of Texas staff in 1975 and immediately became a part-time staffer, Marbridge's first and only professional psychologist-consultant. The men loved having him on campus in an office, so they could take their problems to him. Gentle and firm, he had an enviable knack of calming the most volatile.

In 1975, water well number four was dug, two special education teachers were hired, a Vietnamese couple was employed — Pham Van Ban in the Senior Dorm and wife, Anh Le Nguyet, in the greenhouse; and the Black place west of the ranch was purchased, adding forty-two acres, three houses and some outbuildings to the Manchaca habilitation site.

In 1975 a basic philosophy of the Marbridge Foundation was again proven important — "we want to be our own boss."

From time to time many state and church organizations had approached the highly successful Marbridge directors, asking them to assist in some similar operation.

Finally, Marbridge agreed to take over operation of a Fort Worth community living center for the retarded blind. It worked out very well after the Marbridge staffers took charge. However, they discovered that it was difficult to run a center according to Marbridge standard *and* have other groups, like the Lighthouse for the Blind try to maintain control.

"This was an example of what we have known all along. We can

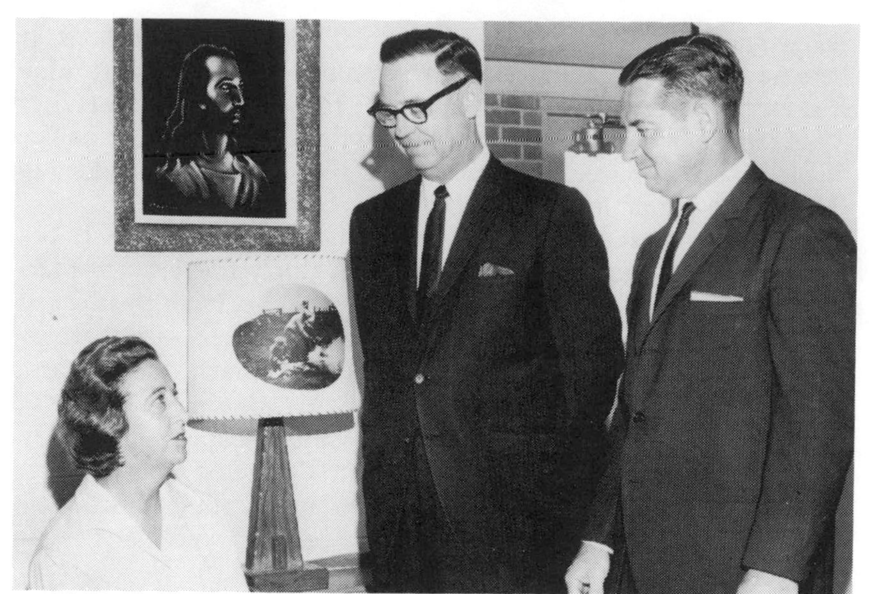

Randolph Walker, right, was the first administrator at Marbridge Ranch. Ed and Marge Bridges, left, hired him in 1956, two years after they founded the facility for habilitation of retarded adult men. This photo was taken in Winters Dorm in the early 1960s.

succeed when *we* alone run it. We find that nobody really understands the Marbridge Plan except those who are involved and have been trained in it. We feel that we must remain cooperative, but we also must be in charge of our own operation, Mr. Bridges pointed out.

Finally Marbridge withdrew amicably from the Fort Worth center.

To round out 1975, the Foundation employed Wyatt Atkins as director of the Austin Community Living Center at its new home in The University of Texas neighborhood. In 1988 Atkins continued as an administrator in the headquarters office on the ranch campus. He, too, had proved to be a longtime, loyal staffer — doing whatever was necessary to "keep things rockin'."

In 1976, a covered walkway was built between Winters Dorm and dining room number three, a third mobile home for staffers was purchased, Pfluger was elected to the board of directors, and Marbridge received an improvement grant from the Texas Rehabilitation Commission to remodel dining room and kitchen in the ranch house.

An important staff addition was Dr. Charles Bell, an experienced specialist in internal medicine and a leading diagnostician. He had served Marbridge as their on-call physician for a number of years. Then in 1976 he found he could devote more time to the Foundation, so he set up a Marbridge Clinic, and came on Mondays, Wednesdays, and Fridays to supervise all health problems and special programs.

It was in 1977 that Richardson Horse Stables, donated by the Sid Richardson Foundation, were built, and David Justin supervised stabling twelve horses.

An experimental adolescent unit for sixteen boys was opened, and lasted some five years. It was discontinued because of lack of referrals.

The Foundation built a medical complex for Dr. Bell located between Winters Dorm and the dining rooms at the old ranch house. It was also just off a walkway which had been constructed to connect Winters Dorm with the dining rooms — mainly to keep the men from getting wet during bad weather. It was an above-ground enclosure of windows, roof and floor. Both the medical complex and walkway have been razed because when the new dining room was built onto Winters Dorm, several rooms were included for Dr. Bell's medical office.

Dr. Bell left his practice at nearby Buda a number of years ago, moving to San Antonio. But he was so absorbed in the Marbridge Plan and loved all the men at the ranch that he continued to come to the ranch Mondays, Wednesdays, and Fridays to oversee the medical needs of the ranch.

Meanwhile, the men launched into the beef production enthusiastically. When the houseparent, Laverne Holden, came on duty one night, she asked the men how their day went. One became excited and said, "Oh, we learned a lot today. We learned how to make steers out of bulls!"

And Mr. B continued to tell parents of prospective ranch residents that "we are not a country club to take your son off your hands. We are a working ranch where our men learn living skills and a trade. They work and play here."

Statistics compiled in 1977 showed that out of 428 men that year, over half were habilitated and moved on to community living centers. Only thirty men were incapable of fitting into the Plan, so sadly they were dismissed to parents or institutions. In 1978, this pattern of success continued:

* *A celebration year.* Marbridge was twenty-five years old and a Texas-size anniversary party was held on the beautifully landscaped grounds at the ranch. What else was served but a Texas-style barbeque.

* *A very sad year.* Dr. Marney, the Bridges' close friend and former pastor, an incorporator and longtime board member, died unex-

pectedly at his home in North Carolina. The entire Foundation, including the residents, mourned their good friend and counselor.

* *A year for the women.* The first group of Marbridge women from the Houston and Abilene halfway houses spent a week of vacation at the Ruidosa lodge and they loved it.

With people and plants, water is a great necessity, so well number five was installed close to the greenhouses. By 1979, the greenhouse operation was becoming "big time." And it meant that the facilities needed to be remodeled, beginning with the first greenhouse. The men who worked the fields harvested a record crop of hay, 8,000 bales. Gary Noonan, current special education teacher, joined the Marbridge staff. Randolph Walker was promoted to director of new construction and maintenance.

Walker supervised building an efficiency apartment adjacent to the fire truck stall to be for ranch graduates going out into communities on their own. In addition, he and the men converted three country homesteads on land acquired the past few years into community living houses, and the men at the Austin house moved in. In addition the low-water crossing at Bear Creek, built nine years earlier, had to be repaired.

For all these years, Mrs. B had been unofficial "supervisor" of volunteers at the ranch. There never was a shortage of volunteers, and their job was mostly to bring fun to the residents. In 1979, the volunteers named themselves "The Marbridge Oak Leaves," taken from the Marbridge symbol which evolved from the many grand old oak trees on the ranch.

On March 30, 1980, a special Founders' Day was observed at which Ed and Marge Bridges were honored. At the height of ceremonies in the Senior Dorm, two bronze sculptures were unveiled, busts of Ed and Marge. The donor was Gregg Ring, and his two sons, Randy and Brian, who were residents of the dorm, unveiled them. The sculptor, Larry Ludtke of Houston, attended and was introduced. After the dorm party, a dinner and reception were held in honor of the Bridges at the Onion Creek Country Club near the ranch.

The interesting sculptures remained in a permanent place in the Senior Dorm, as tribute to the founders of mental health habilitation's greatest operation.

One of the most devastating events, and certainly the most mystifying occurrences ever to happen at Marbridge, came in July of 1980. It was a very hot day; in fact, the temperature reached 100 degrees.

Daniel Fogg, age twenty-five, who had been a ranch resident for seven years, ate lunch in the dining room, and later went to choir practice. He was getting anxious to go home in a few weeks for his birthday. Daniel was last seen about 3:30 P.M. when he was standing near the administration building, a place he liked to frequent to greet visitors. At 5:30 P.M. ranch workers decided Daniel was missing. He had disappeared completely. No trace was ever found; no clues were discovered; no one came forward with any information about his mysterious disappearance.

All law enforcement groups, plus ranch personnel and Daniel's parents, the Donald Foggs of Albuquerque, searched every where in and around the ranch for miles and miles. Daniel was gone.

Since that time, his father has spent thousands of dollars in efforts to find his missing son. He has used every known method of tracking missing persons. He has spared no time limits in this seemingly now hopeless search.

Where is Daniel Fogg? The ranch staff and residents were devastated.

Mrs. B said the subject of his disappearance came up only once at the ranch, and that was at the Christmas program the same year. She cried so much someone had to take her home.

The unexplained mystery of one of her lovable "honeys" remains an all-time Marbridge sorrow — never to be forgotten. The Bridges, like Daniel's family, continue to seek for any clue to his disappearance.

Staff members will tell you that the one fear they always have, even before the Daniel mystery, is finding a man missing. They count continuously.

But Marbridge must go on. In 1981, Robert "Bob" Williamson, a former military finance officer, was employed as comptroller of the entire Marbridge operation. It was a very significant move, as Williamson was being groomed to assume the presidency when Mr. B retired. In 1988 he held the title of executive vice-president.

Williamson was much like Mr. B; he did not require anything of a staffer that he would not do himself. A firm, but gentle person, Williamson agreed with Marbridge staffers that qualifications for working there included first compassion, then love.

The retired army lieutenant colonel arrived with plenty of these qualities. Born in Missouri, he received his first degree from Indiana University where he was in R.O.T.C. thus went into the service after graduation. During one of his two tours of duty in the nation's capital,

Bob Williamson, executive vice president and controller of the Foundation, center, finds it hard to come or go without passing the time of day with several of the men. Above left is Leo Kuritza, and right is James (Bubba) Sellers. If Bubba had his way he'd follow Williamson all day long.

he received a masters' degree in financial management from George Washington University.

He spent twenty-two years in the army, serving overseas in Korea, Alaska, and Vietnam. Williamson and his wife, Joan, have five children. Then as a result of his Far East service, they adopted twin Korean girls. Williamson was most definitely a key person in the expansion and operation of Marbridge. He had a keen insight and a low-key manner which got things done. In addition to being chief financial officer, Williamson spent a lot of time on the road as he was also director of the community living centers throughout Texas. And a third title was "personnel chief," a job he assumed when Pfluger went to the Villa as its chief of staff.

Meanwhile, other events in 1981 included purchase of the Good Times Van, and construction of the fourth greenhouse.

W. L. Todd was elected to the board of directors, as were Robert Jameson of Houston and Pat Davis of Austin.

An independent oil producer, Todd was a regular and generous donor to Marbridge and father of Waren, a resident in the Senior Dorm.

Toward the end of this year, turkey-raising was discontinued as unprofitable. For one thing, the price of feed had risen tremendously. Mr. B was in his 75th year of life, still going strong — and so was his side-kick, Marge, Mrs. B and Mama B (all in one). Marbridge Ranch was an energetic twenty-eight years old. The original dream by the Bridges for a home for their son had reached around the world — and caused some major changes in programs on mental retardation. Their rocky road was a bit smoother now. But the Bridges never stopped dreaming, or joggin' on down that road which they believed God had mapped for them.

Everyone who knew and loved Marbridge and all it meant, could only say: "What next, Mr. B?"

— 9 —

All In A Day's Work

". . . a totally different opportunity for the mentally retarded. A work/life situation geared to each man's individual needs and abilities and programmed to insure each man his own measure of achievement and fulfillment." — from The Marbridge Experience (quarterly newsletter)

Dr. Darrell Mase drove into the gates of Marbridge Ranch on the outskirts of the tiny town of Manchaca, Texas. It had been a long drive from the University of Florida where he headed up one of the first special education departments in the nation. At the small addition to the ranch house marked "office," Dr. Mase met his friend and Marbridge counselor, Dr. John Peck.

He looked around. "But, John, where are the men? I thought they worked on the ranch?"

They walked to the dining room. No men there. They looked around the grounds. No retarded men there.

"Well, get in my truck and we'll try to find them," said Dr. Peck.

They drove toward the fields — up over the top of an oak-covered hill. The hay pasture stretched out before them, and right in the center was a flatbed truck. Busy as bees in the field, helping to stack the bales of hay on the truck were *all* the men of the ranch. An angry black cloud was coming over the Texas horizon; the hay must not get wet. Everyone was helping to get the hay into the barn.

Dr. Mase reacted with pleasant surprise: "This is the kind of thing you can't teach in the classroom."

It displayed very visibly what happens when there is an emergency at Marbridge Ranch. All the retarded adult men came a-running — to help as best they could.

Dr. Mase said this one thing alone was "worth the trip all the way from Florida."

That was over twenty years ago, when Marbridge Foundation was offering a pioneer plan for habilitating the mentally handicapped persons who, up to then, did not have an opportunity to learn skills that would help them lead self-satisfying lives.

Dr. Mase learned that the purpose of the Marbridge Plan was for the men to feel that their work was essential to the survival of the ranch, so they gave their best efforts. In 1988, the dream of Marbridge founders, Ed and Marge Bridges, had come true. Not only was the ranch there for men who needed to work under its supervision, but hundreds of graduates trained by Marbridge were sent out into the community to become wage-earning, tax-paying citizens. In the years succeeding Dr. Mase's visit, he visited many other times and spread the word of the Marbridge concept all over the nation. It was working!

In 1988, Marbridge Foundation was thirty-five years old, a model, non-profit organization that worked magic for the retarded.

Throughout Texas Marbridge community living centers (halfway houses), provided model facilities. When Marbridge Ranch trained a man and he was ready for almost independent living he could move to one of the centers. Some of the men, and women also, came from state and federal referral agencies. Basic for numerous men was the training received in the ranch program.

Over the years, Mr. B, his board and staff set up many different training stations. "It was a trial-and-error situation at first," explained Mr. B. "The main object was to keep the men busy and keep trying to find each one his special spot in a life/work situation."

In the past some of the training stations included dairying, chicken, hog, turkey and game-bird raising and marketing, catfish farming, service station, welding, large scale produce farming, and metal work.

Some of the jobs best handled by Marbridge graduates included janitors, kitchen workers, garden helpers, grocery store aides, warehouse workers, carpenter helpers, electronic assemblers, maintenance personnel, animal caretakers, laundry employees, and babysitters.

Excellent kitchen workers at the Senior Dorm are Jack Little, left, and Bud Kirk, who was one of the first men to come to the Ranch over thirty-two years ago.

There have always been riding horses for the residents' recreation.

Marbridge graduates were hired, because they were reliable, hard-working, enthusiastic workers, insisted Mr. B, or they would not have been sent from the training stations into the community. Included in the training were all types of safety measures and all types of social adjustment skills which graduates needed in inter-acting with others. *Work* was the keystone of the Marbridge Plan.

For this work, even though it was training, and for all chores each man or woman in every Marbridge facility received a regular pay check. This was in accordance with guidelines set for Marbridge by the U.S. Department of Labor.

"All of us at Marbridge have a very positive feeling and a positive attitude to make Marbridge the most successful operation of its kind in the country. We never take the attitude that 'it can't be done'. We have proven many times that the impossible can be accomplished and we are striving to have a continuous attitude and philosophy of this kind as the cornerstone of our endeavors," Ed Bridges said.

For almost twenty years the greenhouses at Marbridge Ranch had been the most visible aspect of the foundation's work plan — to the public, at least — and, have been the principal source of revenue for the non-profit organization.

On any weekend in the year, regardless of the weather, cars lined the road leading to the ten big greenhouses overflowing with flowers and plants of all descriptions. Greenhouse administrator Chris Winslow had twenty-five retarded men of Marbridge Ranch learning and working in horticulture. In addition, Winslow employed four full-time and three part-time workers. Among those were Terry Foster, assistant director. Winslow said the men followed Terry around in his work, learning from him. Many of the men received enough training to be given an independent job in the greenhouse.

Since a high percentage of Texans consider Marbridge Ranch synonymous with "The Greenhouses," Winslow saw this work station as the Foundation's best public relations arm. Winslow said the public saw for the first time retarded men working and training. "They saw what we were doing and how our men were acting. My greenhouse men worked on privilege. If they did not react well with the public, they went back to the ranch campus."

Other privileges included working at the cash register or answering the telephone. Winslow taught them these skills. Carl and Richard could wait on customers and were very reliable in their work. Herbie did not talk much. He was the quiet senior citizen

One of the twelve greenhouses at Marbridge Ranch. From left, administrator of the greenhouses, Chris Winslow; Richard Buckle (in cap) and Ben Yandell. Worker in the wheelchair is Herbie Schumann.

from the Villa, who pushed himself to work in the greenhouse every morning in his wheel chair. Sometimes it took almost an hour for him to get the few hundred yards down the road. But Herbie did not like anyone pushing him, as a rule. Herbie's job for several years was to fill little pots with soil, so a new life could be implanted there, and grow. His contribution to the greenhouse business was important, and Herbie never got bored.

Winslow said his daily problem was just to get all the work and maintenance done involving twelve greenhouses, a small ranch vegetable garden and filling special orders for plants.

Patience was required at all training stations at Marbridge, not the least of which were the greenhouses.

Winslow mixed his patience with humor and compassion. He was very careful not to over exhaust the men. On the other hand, you might hear him yell out, after one of the ranch kitchen men delivered his lunch: "Don't anybody take my cake!"

Many of the ranch pets would congregate at the greenhouses. A long yellow and white cat was usually curled up on the counter beside the cash register. No one bothered him.

One day a person called to ask if Marbridge wanted some kittens.

"How old are they?" Chris told one of the men on the phone to ask. "Four to six weeks." "Ask how many." "Eleven!" "Uh, oh, no, we can't handle eleven. Tell 'em thanks anyway."

Chris Winslow used cats to keep snakes out of garden supplies they liked to eat, and out of the area, in general. Snakes could do damage to a greenhouse operation. A lot of dogs would sleep on the office porch, sometime waking up to greet a visitor or the men. They liked to sleep in the big boxes gathered for packing plants for visitors. One good worker at the greenhouse did not like to talk; he was always humming. If you asked his name, he might say, "I'm Nat King Cole." Winslow said one day he called him, "Hey, Nat King Cole," to which the man replied, "No, my name's Bing Crosby."

Next most popular season to Christmas was, of course, Easter. Thousands of lilies were sold every year at this season. Among the year-long specials at Marbridge greenhouses were rare tropical plants, all kinds of herbs and cacti, evergreens and many types of hanging flowers.

At the greenhouse one also could purchase baskets, pots, plant accessories, birdhouses, wooden plant holders, and a variety of ceramic artwork. The woodwork and ceramic works were made on another part of the campus and sold at the greenhouse.

How did a student majoring in physical anthropology become engrossed in horticulture? Winslow said he came to Austin to study at the university, bringing along a little pot of ivy his mother gave him. It did well in his co-op dormitory. He added other plants, and really got the bug, so to speak. Out riding one day, he discovered Marbridge and saw a very overworked Shelby Collier. Finally, after volunteering on weekends, he told Collier to take weekends off and rest. "I'll come on weekends." And that began his lifetime career. In a newspaper interview recently, Winslow said the retarded men who worked so well with him are all like brothers to him.

Many persons when asked where Marbridge Ranch was would answer: "Oh, yes, I know where Marbridge Ranch is. I buy all my plants there." Customers would drive for miles to pick their plants at Marbridge. One year the greenhouses sold 10,000 poinsettias.

The entire campus, as well as the community living center on its edge, Mabee Village, have been beautifully landscaped. Plants were hung everywhere. All were expertly potted and tended.

In addition to plants and flowers, the greenhouses offered a wide variety of shrubs and fruit trees.

Winslow and his team of teachers explained the details on pruning, planting, watering, pollination, picking fruit, fertilization, and many other aspects of horticulture.

The use of plants and pets for therapy for the handicapped and the aged have been well publicized in recent years. Marbridge Ranch had plenty of plants and pets for their retarded men and their senior citizens. And Winslow had his hands full with twelve greenhouses.

The remainder of the landscaping was mostly under direction of Wyatt Atkins, also an administrator and one who filled a variety of jobs. Once asked if he was going to lunch, Atkins replied, "No, I'll eat lunch next week." He was on his way to see that the men were properly killing ants and fertilizing the lawns. This straight-talking, hard-working young man seemed to be "on call" at all times. In the past he had been a community living center director, the bookkeeper, personnel director, and houseparent. He also handled most of the tax work and Social Security for the residents, and helped work with parents.

Atkins said he could "relate to the men because I grew up with no parents. Marbridge became my family."

A former teacher of water skiing and scuba diving, Atkins also taught all swimming at Marbridge. "I'm a Pisces," he admitted but added that swimming was good therapy for the men; it relaxed them. Some of the ranch residents could not go in the pool due to doctor's orders. No man on seizure medicine could take swimming class.

Since joining Marbridge, Atkins had made a study of the retardation field. "I believe in what Marbridge stands for; it is what the retarded need. Some men need training, not institutionalizing."

Mr. B and Bob Williamson rode herd on all training programs. The concept was this:

In most normal school settings the educational program strived to present meaningful experiences centered around academics — so most people tended to associate school with reading, writing, and arithmetic. Also, people thought of "special education" in terms of remedial academics and a teacher helping students to "catch up." This was not so — at least not at Marbridge.

Here were men who were unable to comprehend many of the very abstract concepts of academic education, but most were very capable of doing quality work with their hands. Therefore a different type of education approach was in operation.

At Marbridge the classroom was the wood shop, the ceramics studio, the greenhouses, the laundry, the kitchens, the fields, and con-

Computer lesson given in classroom by Gary B. Noonan, left, vocational adjustment coordinator, with George Marcus, center, and Travis Pearson.

struction sites. Here many learned skills which would enable them to, in ranch terminology, "head 'em up and move 'em out." Job placement was not unrealistic and it was an excellent goal for the men.

However, there was a classroom. Teacher was Gary Noonan, who actually was supplied by the Austin Independent School District. Noonan, who had been the Marbridge special education teacher for eight years, had seventeen students in 1988. According to the Austin school district, his students had to be under twenty-two years of age, and all individually taught. Most of his students were residents of Mabee and being further trained before being placed in jobs.

Activities which helped the student develop his gross motor skills and muscular coordination were stressed, and meaningful experiences were centered around helping the student learn work skills which he could use throughout his life while experiencing success in his work.

Skills that the students learned from Noonan included how to make change, how to order food at a restaurant (and pay for it), how to recognize directional signs (such as "keep out," "no swimming," "no smoking," "bus stop," etc.). Many of his students learned how to work computers, word processors, and cash registers.

"We practiced, like a drama," explains Noonan. "Then I might take them to McDonalds to see how they would function, or some other place, to put their skills into practice."

Many learned to write home for the first time and how to talk politely on the telephone. If you called Noonan's schoolroom on the ranch campus, sometimes you would get his answering machine recording. But it was not his voice you heard but a voice of one of the students who did an excellent job on the special message. Students felt free to talk with Noonan about problems, their learning desires, anything.

School was held in the mornings, and Noonan spent most of his afternoons assisting the program at Mabee in an effort to help prepare their residents for work in the community. Anyone not already employed and who was living at Mabee Village had to report for classes with Noonan. An important training station at Marbridge Ranch was the laundry, which was a complete commercial-type, all donated by Marbridge Foundation board member, Gregg Ring of Houston.

Ranch men were proud of their ability to work in the laundry. Some fulfilled the important jobs in the Villa and two dorms of collecting dirty laundry then bringing back the clean clothes. Mabee Village had its own laundry.

Theodore Radtke had worked for the ranch laundry a number of years. He was a "marvel" of the ranch. He had the rare mental disorder called ideo-savant, with a high IQ in one portion of the brain, while the remainder of the brain was retarded.

Theodore's brilliant mind was capable of knowing and understanding astronomy — with minute details on facts and figures surrounding this field. He read about it, listened to tapes about it — and talked about it.

The men have had a part in construction of every building on the campus and in landscaping every part of the main ranch grounds.

While the cooking was going on three times a day in ranch kitchens, men were on hand to learn and assist in everything from cooking the pudding and washing the pans to cleaning the ovens.

The kitchen was one of the best training stations, since so many residents of Marbridge community living centers were employed in kitchens of restaurants. The dorms were training grounds for janitorial work. The men learned to buff floors, mop, polish furniture, etc.

Farming as a training station was not as useful as other stations because there was not as much demand for farm workers as for other occupations.

In the commercially-equipped laundry at Marbridge ranch are Theodore Radtke, left, and Charles Puckett.

Field workers — On tractor is Richard Critz, and checking the oil is Doug Payne.

When a ranch resident had minimum training at every work station and he seemed qualified for one of the skills, he was then placed at that station permanently so that he could receive intensive training. In this work situation, he was soon evaluated, and if it seemed he had enough knowledge to live in a sheltered environment, like a community living center, Marbridge staffers got together with his family. They all decided whether to graduate him, or leave him as a ranch resident.

If he remained at the ranch, he usually continued to work where he was best suited and where he felt most comfortable. Thus, he was a part of the work-a-day life at Marbridge.

If it was not advisable for a trained resident to leave the ranch, with its sheltered support, the work then became a station for the man. Each man was pressed to his ultimate in both work and recreation, to make him feel useful and happy and assured of his own worth.

When asked why he liked Marbridge Ranch, one resident said "because we learn so many things." Most others agree, some just say "because we *do* so many things.

Keep them busy! Keep them happy! That's the Marbridge concept — and it's working!

— 10 —

Home On The Range

"If you want to be loved, come to Marbridge Ranch."
— Coach Tex Coulter,
Marbridge Ranch.

A small spotted dog was indignantly barking at the door of the ceramic studio/woodwork shop. The men must have come for a class and forgot to let him in. Pets have been important to any ranch scene, and Marbridge Ranch was no different. A wide variety of pets were spoiled by everybody, residents to staffers. The two dorms, the greenhouses, the Retirement Villa, Mabee Village, a community living center, all had their special pets. A customer might find a cat curled up in a box used for packing plants at the greenhouse office, or another might find a dog asleep under a shrub for sale.

The Retirement Villa had a favorite dog named Sandy who relaxed on a special chair in administrator Pfluger's office. There were some six or eight dogs on the ranch campus, and perhaps as many cats, not to mention the four dainty miniature horses and a dozen or so riding horses. One time the Senior Dorm raised an orphaned lamb on a bottle out behind the east wing. The men were known to become attached to chickens, turkeys, cows, rabbits, and other pets, which provided good therapy for them.

There was a fluffy cat who greeted visitors and staffers at the administration building. When she decided to nap, she had her choice — Dr. Peck's pickup, Mr. B's stationwagon, Wyatt's van, or a visitor's

Board of Directors for the Marbridge Foundation — Left to right are Gregg Ring, Howard Cox, W. L. Todd, Bob Jameson, Pat Davis, former member; Ralph Pfluger, vice-president; Joe Duckworth, J. E. Bridges, president. Seated is Mrs. (Mama B) Bridges, vice-president. Other board members are Jack Wood and Dr. John Peck.

automobile. And just because you saw a doghouse somewhere on the ranch did not necessarily mean that a dog lived there.

One of the architectural "tricks" at the ranch was to camouflage aboveground, unsightly pipes and equipment by building a little "doghouse" above them. To one side of the administration building was such a house — with no door. And to the west side of the Chapel of Love was a small "dogchurch" topped by a steeple. It also had no door. Neither did the one built between two wings at the Villa.

Most of the residents at the ranch and the Villa, were there to stay. Some became trained at the ranch and were able to move outside in society. But for those who remained, the ranch was their home, and everything possible was done to make the residents know — and really feel — that this was their own special home. Following the original Marbridge concept, each person was treated individually and careful consideration was given to fulfill his needs.

Most men felt secure on the ranch, where many called the women staffers "Mama" and a great number "latched on" to a man staffer who became a father-image. Love was important and made the difference between a house and a home.

A secretary at the ranch was walking on her lunch hour to get exercise. As she passed a man on the path, she said, "I think I will just die if I don't get in better shape." He looked so concerned and said, "Oh, no, Mary! Don't die! We love you too much."

The residents took literally everything said to them.

For instance, Walker had to leave a building site one time and go to Austin for a tool. They were pouring cement out behind the old ranch house. He sat one of the men on a chair and told him to watch the cement and not let "any mangy dog get on it." When Walker returned, the man was still sitting and watching the cement. Walker saw turkey tracks all over the wet mixture.

"Didn't I tell you to keep tracks from getting into the cement?" he asked, to which the man replied, "Yes, you told me not to let any old mangy dog get on it — and I didn't."

Residents at Winters Dorm and the Senior Dorm relied on their administrators during the days and the houseparents at night to ease their pain, calm their fears and pat their shoulders — just like all other "mamas." At the Villa, it was Pfluger and the nurse and her aides who cared for the senior citizens' needs, both physically and emotionally.

Said one staffer: "In some ways these people are less fortunate, being retarded, but in other ways, they are more fortunate."

They were completely trusting, and loved unconditionally. They enjoyed small things, and had a lot of people dedicated to taking care of them. They also had plenty of friends and supporters around them. The men were very proud of each other and gave enthusiastic support to each other's goals. On the other hand, the men would fuss and fight from time to time, like all others living under a common roof. Seldom did it come to fisticuffs, but staffers had to break up fights and discipline when necessary. If all else failed, a misbehaving man was sent to Dr. Peck for counseling.

Mr. B said that food was never withheld from a resident. A Marbridge policy was plenty of food — as much as you wanted. Staffers were strict, however, with regard to diets recommended by doctors.

Betty Douglas had been administrator of Winters Dorm for over three years. The dorm was for the younger, more active men. But there was Alfie, who was almost sixty-two. Alfie was a worker and had been at Marbridge for ten years. When he arrived he could not talk at all, then gradually he began "cussing" the younger men, saying how lazy and sloppy they were. They would get on his nerves. Alfie made most of the beds in the fifty-two-bed dorm in a day's time because he did them so well. He also worked in the dining room, setting tables.

Ms. Douglas stressed good dental hygiene, and announced after every meal that all men would have to brush their teeth. Alfie balked. When pressed he got mad, opened his mouth and said, "because I ain't *got* any teeth!"

Alfie, who wore lots of jewelry — rings, necklaces — did not believe in medicine. He would sleep in the barn trying to avoid taking a shot.

"They're a bunch of rowdies," laughed Ms. Douglas, who never had any privacy at all during work hours because at least two or more of her rowdies would follow her when they were not occupied.

She nagged them about shaving — what Mama wouldn't?

Picture Bubba, with his baseball cap on backwards, leaning on her shoulder. And saying, "Mama, will you please help me find my sock?" Of course she would. Bubba was monitored at meals and not allowed desserts until he ate a little something else.

Once Bubba said, "All I want is apple pie. I just want apple pie and a little ice cream."

Someone thought he heard the young man add something.

"Apple pie, a little ice cream, Bubba, and, what, tea?"

"Naw, beer!"

Betty, like all the other dorm employees, felt deeply the responsibility of keeping track of the men. Roll was called at all three meals; at night there was a bedcheck every thirty minutes. Roll was taken frequently when the men were on trips to town.

The ceramics classes were especially busy before holidays such as Christmas and Easter. The teacher had them making pieces for sale at bazaars in surrounding churches or for sale to the public at the greenhouse or thrift shop. All proceeds were turned back into supplies.

The men laughed at one who made Santa Claus's beard brown. Another resident was busy painting an Easter basket, never once looking at it. He was just painting and looking out the window.

Leo was the entertainer at Winters Dorm. Afflicted with Downs Syndrome he cleverly imitated many of the Hollywood and TV stars and most of the Marbridge staff. Leo's special chore was wrapping silverware in napkins for meals. One Easter Leo made a basket for the secretary, and waited by a car for several hours to give it to her. Atkins saw him there and asked him what he was doing.

"I'm waiting to give Mrs. Mary a Easter basket."

Atkins explained to him that he had been waiting at the wrong car.

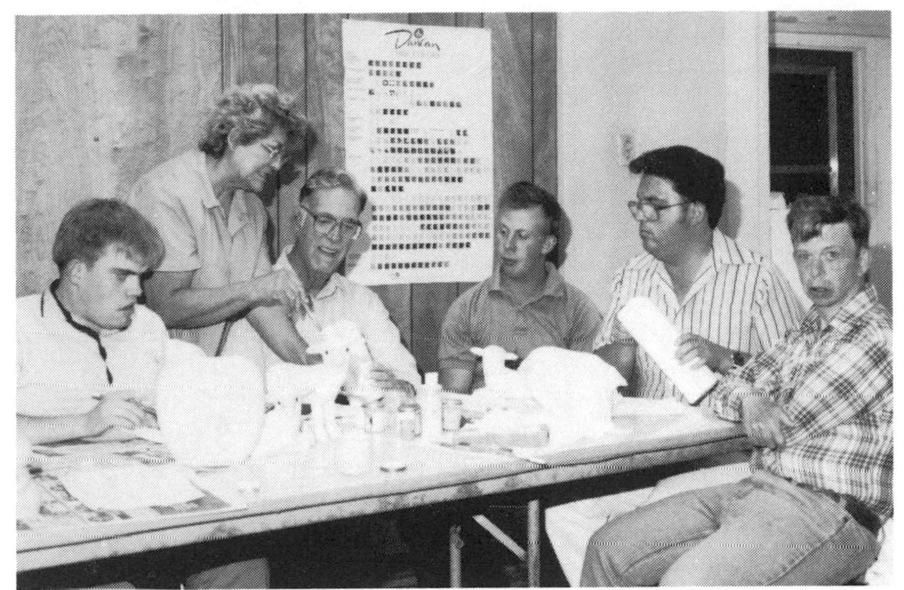

Ceramics instructor, Dora Nielson, works with the men, from left, Brian Higgins, Jim Bridges, Mike Rose, Alex Breceda, and Rudy James.

Mike would say, "I made the pudding"; Jodie would say, "I do pots and pans"; and one of them said, "I'm a bartender!"

Winters Dorm was noisy and full of fun. Most of the men worked in the greenhouses or on the ranch grounds or helped keep their dorm clean.

Ms. Douglas said "you need skates to follow Mark around." Mark was very happy and dependable and emptied wastebaskets at the administration building and did other jobs for them. He knew all that went on at the ranch, and ranged the entire campus.

Most of the men would mind well, as they loved, trusted and admired staff members. Walker said in all his thirty-two years he had had only one man "take a swing at me." Most of the time they listened and tried hard to please.

When a man misbehaved, the staff tried to get to the problem. Was it a medication problem? Was it another person? They would give him many chances, and it was well known that Mr. B required complete proof that the man could not be settled down to Marbridge life before he would allow him to be sent home.

Walker said it was sad when a man had just about learned his way and yet had to be sent home or to an institution. Sometimes it was because of family finances, in spite of the policy of the non-profit Marbridge Foundation to keep tuitions and expenses as low as possible — perhaps lower than any other private foundation in the nation.

How sad it was to learn the circumstances of some of the men's brain damaged. At the Villa was George, a bright college student — a passenger in a carload of speeding boys and girls. He was the only survivor. Also at the Villa was Robert, member of a prominent Austin manufacturing family, who was a top executive and married. Excessive alcoholism destroyed his mind. He was in the last stages of brain deterioration. One man in the Senior Dorm was mildly brain damaged — had a plate in his skull from an accident occurring in adolescence.

Another in the Senior Dorm was riding a horse with his brothers. The horse kicked him in the head during a fall. Some of the men could not read or write, so the staff helped with correspondence. Others had typewriters; one had a computer.

In conflicts between two men, often one of them would write a note about it to the housemother. Sometimes problems were deep-seated and perhaps a few weeks in a hospital was recommended.

Some problems were minor, but unacceptable — such as the two boys who habitually threw things in the commode, like their own eye glasses, pens, pencils, etc.

Recently there was a big disturbance because an administrator made a resident spit out his chewing tobacco. He went to Atkins who said very firmly, "Get your mother to send a letter giving you permission to chew tobacco and then you can chew tobacco." Marbridge's policy was to give every man plenty of chances before dismissing him. Marbridge did not like giving up on a resident.

Shirley Williams, administrator of the Senior Dorm who has been with the Foundation for nine years, said the men would wait at the door for her arrival at 7:15 A.M. and brief her on all activities occurring since she had left the night before.

"We are proud of the behavior and appearance of our men," she said. Most of the residents understood about keeping up the Marbridge image. They, too, were proud of their ranch home.

Ms. Williams said the first thing she did every morning was to see who was sick and to check the schedule of events for the day, including who went to the dentist or doctor, or who was leaving for a visit home. Most of the senior residents, who were physically able, liked to work in the gardens, at the greenhouses, in the laundry, or at the dorm. There was a number of the best softball, track and field

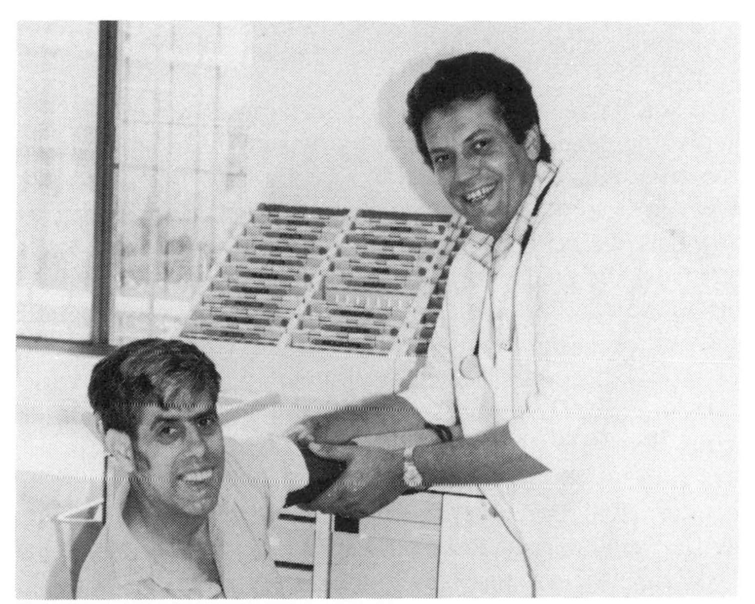

Medical Administrator Gary Brochert with resident, Billy Meadows.

sports stars for Marbridge teams in the Senior Dorm. One can imagine there was a lot of work involved as administrator of forty senior-aged retarded men who were like a houseful of kids.

But like the other staffers, "I'm hooked on the men" and even on her days off or on vacation, she wondered how each one was doing. "They are all so special."

Both senior men and those at Winters had risen to the occasion when called.

For instance, a few years ago a devastating flood caused extensive damage to homes in Austin. Marbridge Ranch was not affected, so Gary Noonan, the special ed teacher at the ranch, gathered up a group of men and headed for the flooded area.

After it was all over, Mr. B received letters from the families helped by the men. "Your charitable contribution of hard-working students and teachers indicate sensitivity, respect and trust," said one Austin man. "The enthusiasm, hard work and ability to work well as a group with definite goals is not able to be described by us . . . it seems obvious to me that Marbridge does an excellent job of developing the capabilities of its finest young men . . . each student enthusiastically followed directions and worked beautifully as small teams" helping several families shovel out debris and cleaning up to get resettled into their homes.

One of Marbridge's greatest satisfactions came from the choral programs presented by the men at various churches, nursing homes, and special events around Central Texas. Another effective community involvement by the staff was to serve on the Manchaca Volunteer Fire Department. Walker had always been the trainer and supervisor of fire-fighters from the ranch. Important were the social adjustment classes conducted by Noonan, which included learning skills like decision-making and peer-control techniques. All the above, believed Mr. B, helped the "boys" in the residents to "grow up and think like men."

Medical needs were supervised by a full-time medical administrator, Gary Borchert, who prior to joining the ranch staff was the first geriatric nurse at the Villa. He moved from the Villa to the ranch after about four years. Borchert followed instructions from Marbridge's Doctor Bell and other doctors for the men and, in addition, was an advisor and support man for the administrators regarding health of the men in the two dorms.

He had an immaculate office at Winters Dorm where he kept detailed files on all residents. Borchert also advised staff members on minor health problems.

And, like the other staffers, he had been known to pinch-hit for a cook, a recreation director or trip leader. He usually took men to town when they needed special medical attention. Borchert said the men really looked forward to trips to the dentist. They talked about it for days, and their friends listened interestingly. Ronnie's job at the ranch was to keep Borchert's office clean. He talked to himself constantly while working. He talked to himself "because it makes my day go by better."

Another resident one weekend washed the medical administrator's special coffee pot. He was very proud of the work and announced that he "used binegar (vinegar) to get the cologne (corrosion) out of the pot."

"The men never complained about the food," said Borchert, except, of course, when he would cut one down on "seconds," putting him on a reduction diet. Mr. B and Mama Bridges put an unmovable "rock" on Marbridge Ranch's foundation: "The men will have all the food they want. And it will be good, wholesome food."

Borchert said nursing residents at the Villa and at the ranch was all the same — and the same as caring for normal persons and older

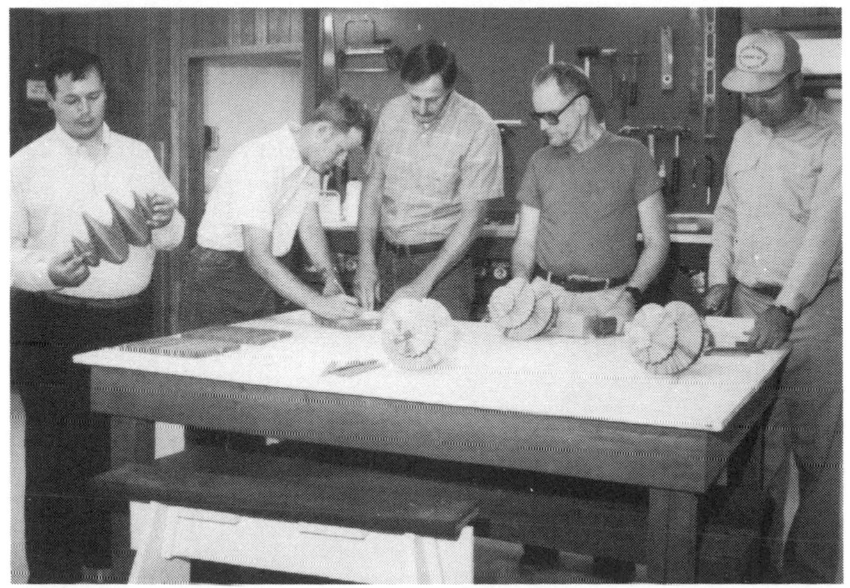

Woodworking teacher, Marcus Shoemaker, center, with at left, Jesse Kirten and Tom Beatty; and at right, Wayman Hammer and Brian Ring.

people. Like Villa administrator Pfluger, he said "they are 'humans' first and retarded second. Their needs are the same."

And who was there for the needs of the men's souls? Sometimes "God" was in the form of an administrator or visitor. But most men seemed to be aware of a Higher Being that they were sure loved them. They sincerely prayed at meals, chapel services, and perhaps in their own rooms. Official religion was handled by churches in the ranch area — the Good Shepherd Lutheran of Buda, the Abiding Love Lutheran in Austin, Manchaca Baptist, Manchaca Methodist, Redeemer Lutheran of Austin, Woodlawn Baptist of Austin. These churches would take turns conducting chapel services on Sunday afternoons at the ranch and would send members to teach special Bible classes or Sunday school classes. On Sundays residents of the ranch and the Villa were taken to the Woodlawn Baptist Church and the Manchaca Methodist Church by ranch van or bus. On Friday, Jewish residents were driven to Temple Beth Israel Synagogue.

Some emotional needs of the men were filled by their friends and peers at the ranch. They developed strong ties and could support one another with needed strengths — just like "normal" people. If they had one quality better than normal persons, it was the ability to accept their lives just as they were.

Said Walker: "They are lovable and attachable, and limited in what they can do. So what if they lack a little bit being a genius — everyone's different."

— 11 —

Emphasis Is On Enjoy

"This is an unusual sort of ranch where we grow a little hay, but mostly grow boys."

Open the door to Marbridge gym, and what would hit you square in the face? Not a ball, fortunately, but laughter and a rousing Sousa march or a western two-step by Willie or Wayland or Reba.

Coach DeWitt (Tex) Coulter said activities were accompanied with music, personal attention, and laughter. Sousa marches were popular.

He explained that "while we range the campus during physical activities, the gym is our headquarters and we try to make it a good place to be."

If a man had a little free time, he usually headed for the gym. One thing Marbridge Ranch was not: *It was not Dullsville!*

There was something to do almost every minute of the day — work, chores, and a lot of recreation. Coulter, a former all-American tackle for West Point, was in charge of recreation, and he said the "emphasis is on enjoy."

He tried to plan activities, coordinating them with the work schedule, that would make every day worth getting up for. In addition, other staffers and some volunteers helped plan and carry out field trips and town trips. It was all under "recreation."

Three years ago the *Dallas Morning News* did a two-page spread in the sports section featuring their pick of the "all-time area high school football team." Their "all-time high school player" was Tex

It's volleyball in the gym for, (left to right) Laurin Otting, Mark Wilson, Bill Carney, and Ronnie Davis.

Coulter, who did his high school playing with the Masonic Home in Fort Worth.

One reason Tex identified with Marbridge Ranch was that he lived at the Masonic Home beginning when he was five years old.

After his high school days ended, and Coulter stood six-foot-five, he entered the army and was sent to West Point, where he was on the World War II powerhouse teams. He moved into professional football and played with the New York Giants for nine years. He left them for a brief year at which time Tex's other talents came into being — he was cartoonist and sometimes sport writer for the *Dallas Times-Herald.* But football lured him back and he played again for the Giants. Later he played for the Canadian League; and when he retired, he and his family remained there where he became one of Canada's top portrait painters. The family moved to Austin where Tex spent a few years in the home-building business when it was booming.

But the challenge at Marbridge lured him in 1981. He filled a number of jobs there, and became full-time recreation director and scout master.

When a staff member once said "The Marbridge men are less fortunate than some, but more fortunate than others," he may have meant

Administrator Wyatt Atkins, swimming instructor at the ranch, in natatorium with some good swimmers. The men are, from left, Billy Blanks, Jaime Reyes, and Willie Faloon (in pool).

that they attended more special events than the average person. They seldom missed a UT football, baseball or basketball game. They attended the circus, movies, rodeos, parades, concerts of various types, dances, and picnics. They visited the Alamo in San Antonio, tourist towns like Fredericksburg, museums, Butter Krust Bakery, television stations, and manufacturing plants. One Christmas the servicemen at Bergstrom Air Force Base near Austin entertained the entire ranch population with a gigantic Christmas party in their honor.

Also under the general category of "recreation" were other parties held at Christmas, Easter, Valentine, Halloween, Fourth of July, everyone's birthday and any others that could be organized.

One Halloween all the staff dressed in sheets and attended the party at the gym. The men loved it. It had been the policy of Marbridge to assign at least four hours work or chores for each man per day, preferably in the mornings. For this, every man on the campus received pay. There was plenty of time for their own choice of hobbies or for recreation — and loading on the big bus for town fun and field trips. The only sports class which Tex did not teach was swimming, which was taught by Wyatt Atkins. Considered recreation were woodshop classes taught by Marcus Shoemaker, and ceramics taught by

Dora Neilson. However, some of the best work in both these classes was sold at the greenhouse, along with the plants and flowers, and at Central Texas churches and bazaars.

Each Marbridge man participated in physical activities to his capabilities.

Bicycling every afternoon looked so fun. A bunch of men on the bikes would wheel up and down the walks and paths on the campus, sailing around corners and waving to friends and visitors. Heading them up was Tex, with his red cap on, and bringing up the rear in good style were the few men on three-wheelers. This was one of the recreational activities that some of the Villa's senior citizens could do. They also liked to go along with the ranch men on the once-a-week bowling trip to town. It was serious business, getting the bowling balls and shoes into a bag and heading out for the alleys. The men would keep a contest going among themselves.

Competition had an appropriate spot in Marbridge activities. It generated interest and enthusiasm, and prepared some of them for the time they would venture back into the normal world to compete for employment.

Included in the competition was an on-going "fight" at any season about which team was going to win in the next game televised or the next one the men would attend. They all had their favorite teams except when asked which was "number One" in football — it was always *"the Giants!,"* Coach Tex Coulter's old team.

Down through the years at Marbridge Ranch, almost every conceivable type of wholesome game or recreational activity had been tried. Some had been popular enough to become permanent sports, like baseball, volleyball, horseback riding, bicycling, hiking, frisbee, and beanbag throwing, tug-of-war, pitching horseshoes, swimming in the heated covered pool, soccer, track, and basketball. Don't forget billards, ping-pong, dominoes, bingo, and weight-lifting.

The most popular with the men was pitch-and-catch. Every time a man caught the ball, it was a victory. Hiking, too, was a recreational activity which the men liked — they saw pretty works of nature and learned to appreciate them. The men enjoyed hiking to the now abandoned three ranch houses which formerly were halfway houses — because everyone called them "haunted." It made for a lot of excitement.

Tex was popular with the men; and they would start yelling out when he arrived at the dorms at mealtime to read off the schedule —

Coach Tex Coulter, in back, with bicyclers, who are (from left) Lee Smith, Dwain Partlow, and Pat Galbreath.

who went where to do what at which time. Tex tried to fit all levels of sports skills among the men.

"I have tried to learn how to get them to do some kind of recreation without bullying them into it. They seldom say 'no'." Whatever he thought they could do best, he inspired them to keep at it.

Instead of declaring, "I want you to . . ." Tex usually would drawl out gently, "Dave, we're going to be riding bikes at 4:00 P.M., sure would like to have you along." Dave usually turned up.

It had been the schedule for the ranch softball team to play the community living center's team about once a week in season. Before Mabee Village came into being in 1987, the center was composed of three remodeled ranch houses on the Marbridge campus — and the teams were about evenly matched.

But when Mabee Village opened, residents of the Dallas Marbridge house went to Austin to live in the new facility. This brought new strength to all teams, and Coach Tex said Mabee really wanted to win. They always did! So early in the 1988 season, Tex asked the Mabee coaches to form a second-string team so that it would give the ranch team a chance to win sometimes and keep their spirit up. It did.

The organized sports, such as volleyball and softball, put the

Marbridge athletes onto the field or gym floor. Men who were the least adept mingled with those who were excellent ball handlers to build teams for competitive sports. There was something for everyone at Marbridge. Many could not perform well in organized sports. But the ones who tried, no matter what, were helped by their teammates. Billy Meadows simply would not participate in team sports, but finally Tex got him to the gym for volleyball one day. After showing him how, he watched Billy serve a perfect ball! Coach said Billy became one of the first always ready for volleyball.

In season, this was the time the men attended some of the UT basketball games. At other times, volunteers or guests presented musical programs or slide shows. For instance, a neighbor of the ranch one time brought wildlife slides and gave an informal lecture. At one point Marbridge challenged any facility anywhere to have available to young persons the great variety of recreational opportunities that the ranch offered on a daily basis. To a man, the Marbridge residents who attended other facilities for the mentally handicapped said that they liked Marbridge much better.

In 1960, Marbridge and six other special schools in the Central Texas area joined together to form the Texas Sports Conference. In succeeding years, Marbridge held the top rank in softball among the south zone of the conference. Individual men also placed high in track. Marbridge men regularly won first places in swimming and track at the state Special Olympics.

Early in the 1960s scouting came to Marbridge with the organization of Troop 403 especially for the ranch men. In 1988 there were forty-one men from the two dorms and the Villa who attended scout meetings once a week, held by Scout Master Tex Coulter.

Two decades after its inception the troop won first in "troop spirit" at the annual fifteen-county Scout-O-Rama. At the event in 1987 Troop 403 received a third place ribbon for its booth featuring conservation and environment. This theme was being pushed in Austin, at that time under a banner of "Xeriscape," which the booth used as its theme. The entire troop helped build and man the exhibit. The booth sign read: "Water and Energy Conservation through Creative Landscape."

The contents of the booth featured beautiful Marbridge plants, trees and flowers and bird houses and feeders made by the scouts. It emphasized proper landscaping by use of these items around one's home displaying how they could help keep useful insects in the yard while repelling pests and harmful fungae.

Mr. B always felt that one of the qualities of "The Marbridge Image" was patriotism. Since scouting was among other things, a patriotic endeavor, a Marbridge troop member presented "the colors" at every official gathering/observation. Most buildings daily raised the flag.

He taught them the boy scout oath and the motto.

"I explained to them what it means to say, 'On my honor I will do my best . . . for my country and myself . . .' and 'I will keep physically strong . . . mentally awake . . .' "

Then he explained that all good scouts should be helpful, kind, cheerful, clean, reverant, among other things, and how all this applied to Marbridge.

"In fact," believed the tall, sixty-one-year-old, physically fit scout master, "the Boy Scout philosophy is a good philosophy for living together — at Marbridge or anywhere."

The Glee club was one of the first activities to be organized at the ranch. Music had long been used as therapy for many illnesses and handicaps. It began in 1955 under the leadership of Mary Peck. This was one of the most active groups at Marbridge. They rehearsed once a week under the direction of Nevin McNulty.

You don't have to be a great singer to be in the Marbridge choir, but McNulty had honed their voices into a group that makes personal appearances at many area churches, other retired facilities and at most Marbridge events. They sang every Sunday afternoon — all year long — during the Chapel of Love's worship service on the ranch grounds. In addition to choral groups, McNulty organized a rhythm band which accompanied many song numbers. The men sang religious, folk, and western songs plus selections from musical shows. He trained nine men for a bell choir and fifteen for a special Chapel Choir.

Previous to McNulty's joining the Marbridge family in 1986, the late Andre Kormany was leader of the Glee Club for a number of years.

When he died, Clive and Carol Robbins were sent down regularly from Dallas by resident Warren Todd's father, W. L. Todd, who was a Marbridge board member. The Todds also donated the rhythm band's percussion instruments. Warren was a longtime member of the choir.

Said this couple: "Music is not an intellectual activity — it bypasses the intellect. Therefore, it bypasses any intellectual dysfunction. This is one reason why music has always had a strong impact on handicapped individuals. Moreover, music affects the whole human personality in a positive way. It stimulates the senses and the mind, demands attention, arouses and nourishes feelings, organizes activity and calls for control and coordination.

"Recent scientific research shows that many areas of the brain are actively involved in attentive musical participation . . . music is one area in which the handicapped can share successfully."

McNulty would begin the mid-week practices of the choir with a prayer, then a stretching exercise to help the men relax. All practices were fun. He might say, "Gentlemen, come on now — where's that Texas smile?"

On and off during the practice hour, the men would be telling him things that have happened since he last was on the ranch. He was patient, kidded, and conjoled them a lot, but said he maintained firm control. "If I didn't, they'd run the choir."

Among the special things he taught was music in sign language; the choir members thought this "a neat thing to learn." McNulty said he believed that music had a unique potential for joy and fulfillment in the lives of the men at Marbridge. Music had been man's inseparable companion throughout history. To be sensitive to music and to respond to it were fundamental to human nature. But if you do not believe this, you should have attended one of the worship services on Sunday afternoon and watched the Marbridge choir perform.

The men's voices and the happiness on their faces was a touching experience. Have you ever really heard an angel sing?

What would a Texas ranch be without horses? Marbridge had nine, so three classes were held on Saturday morning, giving every resident who liked to ride at least an hour of fun.

A couple of the men had their own horses at Richardson stables on the ranch acreage. David Justin, longtime resident, rode with all the classes, assisting when necessary.

Toward the end of each spring on the Marbridge campus thoughts turned toward the high country — and the Foundation's vacation lodge high in the Rockies near Ruidoso, New Mexico. This was a highlight of the year for residents who wanted to go and who had permission of their parents or legal guardians.

Residents went in groups of eight, with two or more staffers, and spent a week in the mountains. Women from the Abilene Marbridge House also spent vacations there.

The other Marbridge vacation spot was directly opposite from the cool high mountain resort in New Mexico. It was a fishing condo at Key Allegro off the Texas Gulf coast. Before the Foundation purchased the condo, the W. H. Kirks, parents of resident, Bud, sometimes made a coastal trip possible for a group of men.

Trips to the coast were made, similar to those going to Ruidoso, each spring and fall: about eight to a group spending a week.

Sometimes a winter trip was made to New Mexico where some men experienced deep snow for the first time. Chris Winslow, horticulture administrator, went on the coastal trip more than any of the other staffers. The men loved fishing, and sometimes a ranch neighbor, Ed Flemming, who owned charter boats, took three or four with Chris on a deep-sea trip.

Eating lots of fresh fish was one of the things the men enjoyed most on the coastal trip. "They liked it family-style," explained Winslow, "all you could eat." Champion eater seemed to be Brian Ring, who was the self-proclaimed "professional plate cleaner." On one such trip they traveled one and a half hours to get to the spot to lower their bait into the Gulf waves. Immediately McLaughlin hooked an eighty pound black-tipped shark. It took much nerve and muscle to get him into the boat — and then he wouldn't fit in the ice chest.

And one time, remembered Winslow, one man caught a barracuda off Rockport, a very rare occurrence. Barracudas seldom stayed in water as cold as the Gulf; they liked warm water, such as found off Florida and the Caribbean. Carl French once snagged a big sting-ray in the bay. The men were interested in looking at it — then threw it back into the waters.

Possibly no facility for the retarded took residents on hunting trips, except Marbridge. Probably because Mr. B and Mama B loved this sport so much themselves that long ago they began teaching qualified men the art of gunmanship. Ralph Pfluger was supervisor of the Rifle Club and taught the men to shoot and hunt. The Foundation had two hunting leases in the Hill Country of Texas, Sandy and Stonewall. Some of the men who did not hunt helped keep the cabins and deer blinds in repair. When they went to work on the property it was a fun camping trip for them.

Maintenance work began in the summer to have everything ready for the opening of Texas deer season in November. Target practice began in early September. Every year they repeated the training, beginning with a .22 calibre gun, and advancing to the rifles. Safety measures were repeated.

Men getting ready for a softball game.

Pfluger said they used many kinds of targets for the men to try to hit during the pre-season warmups. Best to use, he found, was something that made a sound when the bullet hit — like a bucket or plow share or large can. The task was "to ring the gong" which was real excitement.

Pfluger said that it took a number of years for a resident to be ready for hunting. All hunting was done from a deer blind, and a resident was never allowed alone.

Some of the longtime hunters included Robert McLaughlin, Doug Payne, and "Shotgun" Greg Long. Pfluger said Long got his nickname when he was dove hunting with another ranch man. They were sitting under a tree just having a "ball shooting that shotgun, not caring whether there were doves there or not."

Jerry Ladner was a good hunter. Pfluger said it took him over five years to be ready for a hunt. "At first Jerry couldn't hit the shooting pit, much less a target." Once Robert McLaughlin got a deer in spite of the fact that his good "shooting arm" was in a cast and he had to use his left finger to full the trigger. Pfluger remembers one year, he was sitting in a blind with a resident, and a big buck reared its head. Something excited him and he ran to jump a high fence and hit the fence post, knocking himself out. They jumped out of the blind, and the resident got a big deer, shooting him within three feet. They made a pact between them not to tell this story to the others.

The complaint, "there's nothing to do," would not be a valid comment on the lips of any man at Marbridge Ranch and its environs. The spirit of enthusiasm was evident across the campus and across Texas at Marbridge facilities. With all the planned recreation, field trips, vacations — mixed with hard work and skilled training for jobs — there were many Marbridge men and women who could say their life was the "good life."

— 12 —

Courage to Face the World

"They had their first chance at establishing themselves as self-supporting, tax-paying citizens. And they were succeeding."

In the busy, steamy kitchen at the Veterans Administration Hospital in Houston, a thirty-eight-year-old dishwasher kept his mind on his job. He had missed very few days of work in the past sixteen years. He was never late. He did a good job.

When he was nineteen, he entered Marbridge Ranch for retarded men in Austin and spent two years in their training program. He did so well that he was then transferred to the Marbridge community living center in Houston. Counselors and staffers worked with him at that facility several months, then helped place him in the dishwashing job at the VA hospital, for which he was paid $4.81 per hour.

Sixteen years later, Ricky Williams was proud of his record that brought home $7.36 per hour. Marbridge House taught him how to save his money and conduct his own banking. He had numerous C.D.s and a large savings account.

In addition, he had matured in his personality, no longer had fits of temper, was careful of his language and appearance and was a member of the Boy Scout Explorer Group.

Ricky found happiness, one of many such persons habilitated by the Marbridge Foundation. He was a wage-earning, tax-paying citizen.

At Abilene's Marbridge House for women Gloria Nowlin, age fifty-three, was a loving and friendly person who worked at the Hen-

Houston's Marbridge House — it keeps growing and growing.

drick Medical Center as a maid for seven years. Gloria did not walk until she was thirteen years old. She got around in her home on her knees. When her father brought home a dog, Gloria was entranced. The dog followed her all day, jumping and running. She soon began to imitate him — and within months she was walking correctly, following her dog everywhere. Finally came the running and jumping with her dog-teacher. Her household was happy, and so were Gloria and her dog. Now she needed to catch up on her learning.

At Marbridge House she attended adult education classes, hoping to learn to read and write. She was a satisfied, well-rounded person who loved attending church, shopping with the other women from the facility and learning how to cook. Like Ricky, she had become a wage-earning, tax-paying citizen.

Karen Lewing had been at Marbridge House in Abilene since 1981. And since 1981 she had worked for Red Lobster Restaurant, preparing shrimp for the cooks. Her fellow workers praised her. She walked with a slight limp, having been crippled at birth. She did not have full use of her right hand and had a speech impediment. But she, too was working hard in adult education classes, hoping to receive her GED in 1988. The Marbridge staff taught her how to save her money.

She used some of it for a trip to Colorado to visit her mother and brother. Karen was a happy, wage-earning, tax-paying citizen.

Thirty-eight-year-old William Robert had been in the Houston Marbridge facility for fifteen years, which was the same number of years he had been doing a good job at Scott Antique Furniture refinishers. When the boss was away, he learned to handle the business. William was a warm and caring friend of others in the habilitation center.

Like most of them, he took his job very seriously, was seldom absent and always on time. He worked the "extra mile" when necessary, and his employer had come to depend on him.

William accumulated C.D.s, knew how to handle his own checking account and every first of the month paid his own expenses at Marbridge.

His brain damage condition was not readily apparent, but he felt he needed the Marbridge support in his life. William became a happy, self-supporting, wage-earning, tax-paying citizen.

In addition to working for the Houston House, David Weeks had worked for the VA Hospital for seventeen years; Dennis White was employed by Warren Electric Supply as a security guard, carrying a whistle instead of a gun; and Jerry Spencer worked as a janitor for the City of Houston Fire Department.

Stories could continue — stories of people who showed the world what it took to succeed, even while overcoming mental and physical barriers that would defeat most of us.

Long ago Marbridge, founded by Ed and Marge Bridges, differed with this theory. They set out to prove that some mentally retarded individuals could be trained and employed in the community. They proved right!

Their first facility, Marbridge Ranch, was founded in 1953. When the first few men had learned skills which seemed adequate for use in the "outer world," the Marbridge Foundation wondered what to do with them. They needed to go out into the community and become useful citizens.

Then, too, there were many on the ranch waiting list that had applied to take their places — to learn what the graduates had learned: how to cope with life and develop their highest potentials. No other facility offered then what Marbridge Ranch offered.

So while mental health professionals were talking about possibilities of community living centers for young adult mental retardates, weighing the pros and cons, Ed and Marge went ahead and established not one, but several, centers in key cities in Texas. In 1961, Marbridge set up the Houston House for their proud graduates.

Some of the men who moved on from Marbridge Ranch returned to their family homes and received help in finding acceptable places in the community from relatives or hometown agencies. If not, Marbridge offered a more elaborate plan in the network of state Community Living Centers, popularly termed "halfway houses."

These centers made it possible for greater placement opportunities than could be arranged directly through the ranch. Homelike centers in downtown residential areas, the houses were always filled to capacity with residents who found harmonious surroundings that promulgated working, sharing, and living adult lives together. The most successful among the residents, in time, could move on again to become totally self-sufficient wage earners and citizens in their chosen communities.

Marbridge drew on many professionals in their residential training operations, but down-to-earth philosophy of good food, social adjustment, recreation, training, church and busy days for the retarded appealed to business people, professionals in education/rehabilitation and to parents.

The old no-nonsense attitude of "let's get on with it" based on private enterprise, combined with management skills, made Marbridge Foundation a success from the start.

After exploring all angles of the new concept of halfway houses for retarded young people who were not ready to go from institutions into independent living, Ed and his board picked Houston as a site. It met all qualifications.

It opened in 1961 with Mr. and Mrs. Frank Sawyer as directors. There was a formal dedication of the large house at 5219 La Branch Street. Beginning with fifteen residents, mostly graduates of the ranch program, in 1988 eighty-four men were housed in a dormitory built on the same property.

Said Mr. Bridges, "we were always short on facilities and felt we needed to keep all community living centers modern and roomy."

With his fund-raising abilities and donations from other foundations and from individuals — plus an occasional government grant — Marbridge Foundation had always been able to make its dreams of expansion come true.

At the Houston House Mrs. Sawyer cooked and ran the home as a mother. Mr. Sawyer worked as guidance counselor and sought assistance in finding the men jobs from the Texas Employment Commission. Both said they treated the residents as if "they were our own children."

Administrators and staffs at all three of the current, large Community Living Centers at Houston, Abilene, and Austin followed this concept.

Within two years of founding, the Houston facility had lots of feedback from employers who praised the work of the men. Some of the residents had already saved money; one was sending money home each week to a widowed mother.

Finding steady employment in a tight job market challenged anyone who was out of work — but for the mentally retarded, employment meant much more than holding down a job. For many, it was the key to a lifelong goal of independent living.

Thanks to Marbridge and its community living centers and to stalwart employers of the handicapped, more and more mentally retarded adults were turning that key. Reasons for the success of the Marbridge house in Houston was due, not only to the house, but to an interested and cooperative community, including employers, the news media and the public. In 1988, newspaper, radio, and television stations covered the saga of Safeway Stores and Houston Marbridge. Safeway had hired many Marbridge residents and had been very complimentary on their performances.

The Marbridge Foundation presented four Safeway managers in Houston special certificates of appreciation for their "cooperative and generous help" in paving the road to independence for handicapped people. One of these people was David Foltz, who had worked several years as a courtesy clerk. Previously, David had spent most of his fifty years in state schools for the mentally retarded before entering the Marbridge program.

His manager said he was a "people-oriented guy who loves to talk. He has many friends among our customers and is well liked by everyone . . . I consider him one of my greatest public relations people and a real asset to my store."

Houston newspapers regularly ran feature stories on the men of Marbridge and their achievements. One was on Ricky Gentzel, who had suffered encephalitis when he was a pre-teen; and when he came out of a thirty-six day coma his right side was paralyzed and his right arm drawn up tightly to his face. He could not talk or swallow. Through rigid therapy and special education, it took Ricky only three years to complete the school courses through sixth grade. But the tragedy struck again in an automobile accident and Ricky sustained injuries to both legs. Therapy work began again. Ricky had been a resident of Marbridge for thirteen years. Through its support and his own determination, he was able to hold down a job as pantry aide in the Westin-Galleria Hotel for over eleven years. The Westin Hotels honored him with the Thurston-Dupar Inspirational Award which they gave annually to an employee.

Ricky played on his church volleyball and soccer teams. One year he completed a twenty-five-mile walk for the March of Dimes, and later a twelve-mile-walk, helping his roommate who was "less fortunate."

During his training at Marbridge House, he discovered he had artistic abilities, and sometimes the Galleria would ask him to design posters for their parties and advertisements for their promotions. He joined the hotel chain making $2.45 per hour, and later made $5.10 per hour.

With the new training facility in Houston, Marbridge Plan was working — again!

Many agencies, like Opportunity Center in Houston, and many parent groups were referrals for Marbridge. Most men were aged eighteen to twenty-two years and had I.Q.s ranging from 58 to 78.

The Texas Rehabilitation Commission took a strong interest in the Marbridge program from the beginning and were referring residents to them. Most of them worked out. Mr. Bridges believed that the Texas Rehab program was the best state agency of all agencies, working effectively for the most good.

TRC paid the tuition for the first few months at a Marbridge facility during the trial period and until the resident would become self-supporting.

TRC was a vital force in furnishing funds for the training of many men and women with all types of handicaps. Their efforts many times paid its way over and above their cost to the tax payers.

According to a letter sent by Director Ron Trull of Rehab's training and placement unit a few years ago to Louis Willoughby, then director of Marbridge Houston House:

> The excellent services provided by your facility have come to my attention. Our central office computer indicates your facility successfully rehabilitated thirteen TRC clients in fiscal year 1986. This is the highest number of rehabilitated citizens of any residential facility

> in our Region IV (Harris County). Also, you had the highest success rate (100%) of any residential facility in Region IV. I wish to congratulate you and your staff for a job well done.

Statistics from the Houston facility in 1981 showed that the ninety residents there paid to the government in social security, income tax and sales tax, $90,600. They had in savings accounts, $48,043.55; and in bank certificate of deposits, $54,600.

In comparison, the Texas Rehabilitation Commission paid in the same period for maintaining thirteen men in one of their halfway houses, $90,508.00.

Stated one official source, "This demonstrates the economic worth of habilitation in dollars. The worth in pride and self-esteem cannot be told in dollars."

The Wall Street Journal devoted a lengthy story on nationally known companies who employed the handicapped and who recommended this policy.

Headlined "Faced With Shortages of Unskilled Labor, Employers Hire More Retarded Workers," reporter Roger Ricklefs explained that many companies and agencies felt hiring the handicapped was well worth the effort.

> Faced with shortage of reliable unskilled labor, major employers say they are expanding efforts to hire the retarded. Marriott Corp., for instance, already has well over 1,000 mentally handicapped workers and says the number is growing . . .
>
> If they are placed in the right job and thoroughly trained, the retarded are effective and motivated workers, employers say.

The story told about the Yankee Steamer Inc., an office cleaning concern in New Jersey. Owner Kevin Ettinger stated "they are slow in the beginning, but they catch up. With unskilled teenagers, the absentee rate would be three or four times as high." Yankee steamer counted fifteen retarded people on its staff of twenty-one, and planned to add more.

The *Journal* story went into a new and successful policy of hiring more seriously retarded workers by many companies. Of 2,000 people whom the Association for Retarded Citizens placed in full-pay-and-benefits jobs one year, nearly 400 were "moderately" or even "severely" retarded, said Ricklefs' article:

> Even with less retarded workers, the agency helps organize jobs into fixed routines. In a Manhattan office building, employment-train-

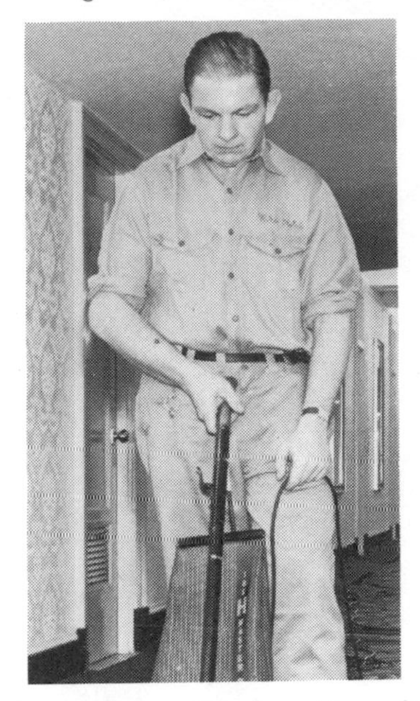

Among the better jobs for residents of Marbridge Community Living Centers are as janitors and kitchen helpers. They take great pride in their work.

ing specialist Brenda Kantarian establishes a route for cleaning hallways. She accompanies a new worker on the job, full-time, for several days."

According to *The Wall Street Journal* article, Kantarian declared it works. One retarded janitor for her said "If I stick to the route, I don't get confused." He kept his floors immaculate.

Employers developed numerous techniques to solve work problems. To help workers sort out laundry, Marriott sometimes used different-colored bins for various sizes of sheets and towels.

The association for Retarded Citizens even placed a Maryland woman with an IQ under thirty (100 is average) in a job cleaning offices. It equipped her with a Walkman-like device, the story said, "That plays music. Periodically, a voice interrupts the music to ask if she has emptied the waste basket and ashtrays and to remind her to move on to the next office. Elsewhere, McDonald's Corp. assigns a woman with an IQ of thirty-six to spend all day making French fries — a task she could grasp, even though it involved forty-seven steps . . ."

Many employers said they were hiring the mentally disabled because of their dependability and willingness to stay on the job, continued the *Journal* story:

> Southland Corp., the Dallas-based operator of 7-Eleven convenience stores and other enterprises, is sharply expanding efforts to hire the retarded, largely to ease the growing shortage of workers who will stick with low-skilled jobs . . .
>
> Woodward & Lothrop Inc., the Washington, D.C. department store chain, says one retarded worker has been washing pots and pans in the kitchen for six years. "Normally we would have a turnover of two or three a year in that job," says the company's manager of personnel and community services. Retarded workers "don't get bored as quickly," he says, adding, "We don't yet know the full potential of a retarded person."

Ed Bridges was a businessman by training and long experience. His experience with the mentally retarded was with his son and with his participation in numerous groups interested in mental retardation. But the above ideas mentioned in the *Wall Street Journal* article came to him many years ago.

He gave up a lucrative career in the furniture business in Austin when Marbridge Ranch began expanding — and devoted his full administrative energies to the Marbridge Foundation. The original ranch expanded into the community living centers and, later, into a retirement facility for retardates.

Mr. B received a letter from Richard Nelson, who entered training at Marbridge Ranch when he was seventeen, leaving it two years later for Houston Marbridge House. He spent eight years there, but for the next sixteen years was on his own in independent living in Houston. In the letter Richard recalled how homesick he was during his first couple of months at the ranch. He was glad he survived and went on to achieve normal living. Richard sent a contribution to the new Mabee Village in Austin in honor of Randolph Walker's many years on the ranch staff. He said he did not forget those early learning years.

For eight summers Richard spent his two weeks' vacation in the heart of Mexico at a mission. He taught the children such skills as gardening, and loved seeing his special children each year. Of course, he had learned Spanish.

Now, according to his letter to Mr. B, he was also studying German. He asked Mr. B to tell Ralph Pfluger that he had learned that "pflug" means "plow," and that surely Pfluger must be "a plower."

Soon after the opening of the Houston facility, the Bridges began receiving calls from parents of retarded women who had heard of Marbridge and who also needed a place of habilitation for their daughters.

It was in 1967 when Ed and Marge Bridges, above, answered a need — and founded the first Marbridge community living center for women in Abilene.

Recognizing this, the Foundation opened the Abilene House for occupancy of thirty women in 1967. By 1988, it had been expanded to accommodate over eighty women. It also was fulfilling the hoped-for goals of the Marbridge dream.

Mr. B said he had always been especially proud of the Abilene Community Living Center. Like the ones in Houston and Austin, it had been kept modern and expanding.

In the beginning, Abilene's Marbridge House was located on 17th Street, but in 1973 the Foundation purchased St. Ann Hospital and renovated it for comfortable use by the handicapped women and the staff. Incorporated in this complex was a wing for thirty women, a large recreation hall and a rear unit where once the Catholic sisters of the hospital lived but now accommodated ten advanced women who held a seniority status. Included in the complex was a covered swimming pool for year-round swimming donated by a group of parents.

Teachers from the Abilene Independent School District would come to Marbridge House three days a week to teach residents who wished to attain their GED degrees and high school diplomas. The West Texas Community Living Center also provided such services as audiology, speech and language, physical therapy and occupational therapy. Ready on call were a psychologist, social worker, and registered nurse.

Gena Oldham was a forty-one-year-old resident who had been at the Abilene facility since 1981. Previously, since age eleven, she had been in the Austin State School and Mexia State School.

She learned quickly at the Abilene House and soon was employed by the Red Lobster restaurant where she had worked happily for some seven years.

Bessie Arnold, formerly of the Lufkin State School, had been at Marbridge Abilene for over eighteen years. For almost the same length of time she had been a good employee of Abilene Christian University's bakery department.

The Dallas Marbridge House for men opened in 1967 and operated like the Houston facility. In an expansion, it was located in 1972 on Gaston Avenue, then in 1987 this site was put up for sale and the residents moved to the very exciting Mabee Village. This was the newest facility opened just off the Marbridge Ranch campus and housed residents of the Austin and Dallas centers. In an innovative move, it was also opened to women. Administrator Benny Howard said the coeducational facility was working very well.

Marbridge House was first placed in downtown Austin in 1970, and expanded to larger quarters on San Gabriel Street in 1975. Director at that time was Wyatt Atkins, who later served the Foundation as an administrator in the headquarters office on the ranch.

Sometime after 1975, Mr. Bridges and the board began looking elsewhere for a suitable location for the Austin Home. City taxes, rental prices, utilities and other factors made the idea of placing it near the ranch seem practical.

The Foundation earlier had acquired three adjacent properties to the ranch, so the three country homesteads were converted to halfway houses. The Austin residents went "country" and moved into what was called "The Marbridge Residences" in 1979. Eight years later this facility evolved into Mabee Village.

An unsolicited letter from a neighbor of the downtown Austin Marbridge House was printed in an issue of *Austin American-Statesman:*

> I have no ax to grind, but I do want to add a little knowledge, based on personal experience, to the body of material on the question of whether or not residences for the mentally handicapped should be placed in neighborhoods.

For a short time, a halfway house for mentally handicapped young men was situated in a large house next door to mine.

The young men living in this establishment were very good neighbors to me. They were pleasant, friendly, not unduly noisy. When a baseball or football flew over my wall or lodged on my roof, the young men always asked my permission before they retrieved it. When I forgot and left my car lights burning at night, my handicapped neighbors came and told me about it. We got along fine.

I hope this information will be helpful.

W. H. CRAIN

All the community living centers proved to federal and state agencies that it was not only possible to habilitate some mentally retarded persons, but that it was practical to operate such programs. It could save the government agencies thousands of dollars annually. Private enterprise was paying its own way, Marbridge-style.

So it was for residents of the community living centers. From the beginning, they learned that, as much as possible, it was very commendable to pay as much of their own way as possible. Training residents to manage their money was of utmost importance in the Marbridge plan.

Residents "banked" their paychecks with the director of their house, drawing on it for such things as clothes and shopping trips. When their savings reached a certain level, the director set up an individual savings account at some bank for the resident. Each man or woman had been considered individually for job placement, with consideration of his or her vocational aptitude and preferences of jobs. They were completely and properly trained for whatever job the centers found for them.

"Many retarded persons need most of all a sense of success gained, most often, from holding the same job over the years. They do not become bored as normal persons tend to do. For these people staying put is more rewarding than moving up on the wage ladder," according to Mr. Bridges.

Some of the jobs most often held by Marbridge trainees were janitor, shipping and receiving clerk, dishwasher, kitchen helper, bus boy/girl, car washer/polisher, carpenter's helper, electronic product assembler, nursery and landscape assistant, food server in cafeteria, warehouse laborer, apartment maintenance man, animal caretaker, laundry employee, and babysitter.

Residents were encouraged not to have too many social activities,

Some of Mr. B's "lovely young women" at Abilene's Marbridge House. In back row, center, is Mrs. Yvonne Cheek, administrator of the facility.

which would interfere with proper sleep in order to perform well on their jobs.

Mr. Bridges said it was not his wish "to rush residents through the community living center with the idea of placing him or her in independent living too quickly. The individual should probably stay in the facility for at least one to two years, during which time he was trained in handling money, use of leisure time, problems of socialization, proper health and dental care, etc."

At the end of this time, each resident was evaluated carefully. The director had strict guidelines to follow in deciding if, at this time, the resident was capable of surviving in a completely independent living situation. Some residents did better in a community living center, where it was best for them to remain during their entire working life.

It took unusual courage for a man or women with handicaps to make that giant step into the normal world and ask for this world to accept them and give them a chance. Marbridge House staffs helped bridge this fear and build needed courage. The courage had always been there; it just needed an understanding push.

Sharon Stevens and Gary Hays' lives were salvaged in Marbridge House. They met in the Houston facility, fell in love, married and went into that world and established their lives together in happiness.

For many years, Sharon's father, Clovis Stevens, now deceased, was director of first the Marbridge Dallas House, then the Houston House.

During his tenure with the Marbridge Foundation, he often was called to act as a trouble-shooter adviser to the other community living centers. Also during their years in Houston, he and his wife operated a Marbridge House for women. When the Abilene facilities were expanded the Houston women residents moved out to West Texas. Mrs. Stevens was still on the Houston staff in 1988.

Among satisfied and willing employers of the handicapped in Houston was the Rice Hotel which said of these employees: "they are an excellent source of stable, capable workers."

Featured on a 1965 cover of the hotel's monthly newsletter, "The Rice Roomer," was Phillip Thompson, who had performed well in the housekeeping department. Phillip's picture also was used in a conference of social workers in Texas as an example of what a halfway house can accomplish. A Houston House resident for twelve years, Bobby L. Drake came from the Lufkin State School. He held several jobs in the Dallas area, but was an unsatisfactory worker because he would display bad temper — and sometimes walk off the job.

With the guidance of the Houston Marbridge House, his temper was quelled, he stopped his crying spells and became a good resident, obeying all rules and performing well.

Age thirty-one, Bobby had been in the dietary department of the Veterans Administration hospital for five- and one-half years, and his salary increased from $4.80 to $6.83 per hour. Bobby and others of the Houston House men flew to Florida the summer of 1987 to Disney World — strictly on their own. This was quite an accomplishment! Bobby was looking forward to going to England to visit his grandmother. He had money in the bank for such things, and was another happy, wage-earning, tax-paying citizen.

It took just six years for Marbridge Houston House staffers to "mold" Richard Fernandez into a secure, good-feeling, helpful young man. Previously he had left special education classes in the 10th grade, been very insecure and had no interest in either his own self-image or anything going on in the world about him. It took constant attention from the staff and supporting volunteers to transform him into an outgoing and happy person. He held a job in the dietary department of the Veterans Administration Hospital in Houston for four years. Richard was a trophy-winning member of the House bowling league team and of the Explorer Boy Scout troop. He had a savings account and some C.D.s and was also a happy, wage-earning, tax-paying citizen.

Morris Knudson, age sixty, went to Marbridge Ranch from a state school where he had spent most of his life. About 1962, he was trained and well adjusted so he moved to the Houston House where he found employment. Morris had been working as a staff member for thirteen years. He was on the midnight to 8 A.M. shift. Among his jobs was fixing the sack lunches for the residents who worked out in the community, helping serve breakfast and assisting the men in getting off to work. Also at Houston and proud of their seventeen years on the same job were Paul Biley and Jimmy Dingler, both employed by the Sakowitz Department Store.

Abilene House resident Sandra Moore, coming from the Houston facility, worked from 1981 to 1986 at the Holiday Inn in housekeeping as a maid. She was a hard worker, and soon found another job as housekeeper at the Embassy Suites Hotel. Since Sandra loved desserts, the other women at Abilene help her watch her diet. Sandra also gave herself insulin shots each morning. She lived in one of the Marbridge duplexes, and kept everyone in a jolly mood. She had money to travel to Houston, Vernon, and New Mexico. At age twenty-nine, she was a very active and dedicated church worker.

Gloria Flores went to the Abilene House from the Abilene State School in 1978. She had been abandoned long ago by her family. Although she had a hearing problem, wore a hearing aide, and had a speech impediment, she acquired many friends at the Abilene complex. The staff called her one of the neatest persons in the House. She worked effectively for La Hacendia Restaurant, Holiday Inn, and a grocery store.

These individuals and all the trained and working residents of Marbridge's community living centers won a large victory for the mentally retarded all over the country. Their success was a notable achievement for them and for the Marbridge Plan.

Where once Mr. Bridges and his directors were laughed at for believing that some retarded could be taught to live in normal settings, the scoffers now came to the Foundation for advice.

Success of the men became evident at their first facility in Houston after the first year. The men were happy, employers were happy, parents were happy. The Plan was working!

In line with the Marbridge Foundation's basic philosophy of keeping their residents busy as possible, all men and women worked. If they did not have outside jobs, they helped with house chores, sweeping, mopping, washing windows, etc. The administrators assigned these work stations.

"When a person sits around, he or she deteriorates," said Mr. Bridges. The eighty-year-old founder of the Marbridge Plan practiced what he preached.

He put in a full days' work in the office on Marbridge Ranch. He kept constant "tabs" on what went on within the Foundation and out in the community living centers. He solicited and got complete cooperation from every person involved in the Marbridge's operation.

Mr. Bridges could be heard in the hall talking with one of the residents at the ranch. "Well, did you get that rocking chair fixed?" Or one might catch him in his office, practicing usage of the new video camera the Foundation purchased for entertainment and promotion. He did not expect anyone to do what he could not do.

He was the first one to explain that his Foundation operated entirely as a private, non-profit organization. And that is why the Marbridge Plan had become so strong." For sure the world judged by results obtained. Marbridge got results!

— 13 —

A Home — At Last!

"One dream after another has come true."

A small hand knocked on the big door which was decorated with the picture of a smiling Halloween pumpkin. The door opened wide, and the small witch looked up at the tall witch.

"Trick or Treat!"

Other costumed witches and goblins stuck their heads out from the inside, laughing and mumbling. Some also yelled "Trick or Treat." The big witches and goblins had been working for weeks, and waiting anxiously for the fun of Halloween. They loved little children. They were residents of Marbridge Retirement Villa which was located on a portion of the famous Marbridge Ranch for retarded adult men, just one of the facilities operated by Marbridge Foundation. Halloween was another celebration for the retarded senior citizens. Volunteers and staff at this innovative retirement home observed every occasion possible — from St. Patrick's day to Christmas and, of course, every resident's birthday. When they ran out of special days, they came up with a Hawaiian luau or a Mardi Gras celebration.

With the on-coming of a special occasion, the Villa became gaily decorated from kitchen to every one of the twenty-six rooms, where fifty-two old-timers felt secure in that they had found *A Home — At Last!*

The Villa opened in the spring of 1983, and was heralded as a retirement "showplace of the nation." This was because nowhere else in the nation was there a similar facility, a retirement/nursing home for the retarded.

Marbridge's "showplace" — The Retirement Villa.

Why not a pioneer concept? The non-profit Marbridge Foundation dealt in establishing pioneer facilities and proved that the retarded, in many areas, could find a security and happiness that previously had not been attainable for them.

For those in the twilight years of a retarded life it was customary to move into some nursing home with feeble, senile, often bedridden patients for their only companions. But Marbridge Retirement Villa recognized that an aged retardate could have as many as fifteen or twenty years of living before becoming this helpless.

So in the Marbridge tradition of keeping their handicapped men at the ranch as busy as possible, and pushed to their maximum achievement, the Villa offered a wide variety of activities for their residents.

Keep them busy! Keep them happy! That was the goal of Ralph Pfluger, who had been with the Marbridge Foundation since 1961 and was the only administrator of the retirement Villa. Pfluger had served in almost every capacity for Marbridge Foundation. As Villa director, he was vice-president on the foundation's board of directors.

He had a keen sense of the special needs required by his residents and also a good sense of humor. Both were necessary to perform as a staffer or administrator at the unusual facilities which coped with out-of-the-ordinary problems — like one cold day when a male resident came back from the synagogue wearing some lady-worshiper's fur coat.

A few years ago Marbridge found that some of the men who had been residents of the ranch since its early years were reaching retirement age, when they could no longer keep the busy pace at the ranch. What were they to do with them?

Founder and board chairman Bridges said "We operate as a retirement facility for that individual who needs a less competitive life and requires some supervision; and as a Level III nursing facility for those retarded men and women whose health needs are such that they require nursing care."

Since Marbridge's inception it had been necessary to keep building, trying to accommodate those persons who wanted to enroll for the training program. So it was, also, with the Villa.

Five years old, in 1988, it had on the drawing board a new wing to house thirty-two new retirees. Pfluger said he had a waiting list at all times, and they came from throughout the world. Of his fifty-two men and women residents, fifteen were not retarded. Pfluger laughed and said that these gave the most trouble — sixty percent of the normal group were women and "these women took sixty percent of our time.

How did the Villa happen to accept applicants who were not retarded? Families in the Marbridge Ranch area, near Manchaca, heard about the retirement facility and wanted their parents in a happy facility — and one close to them. The Villa was perfect! Most of them already knew about Marbridge Ranch's successes; many knew Mr. Bridges personally. So they were accepted as vacancies occurred.

Every resident was "a human being first, and retarded second. That's the way we treat them. The older persons are a little more fragile than younger ones . . . not only are their skin and bones soft, but they have soft feelings, too . . . we try to give them something to lean on at this time of life," Pfluger pointed out.

He and his staff tried to trace the "pattern" of residents' likes and dislikes and abilities, so they could see what activities would inspire them and where they would fit in.

For instance, Bea, who ran the thrift shop, came from a nursing home where the order-of-the-day was watching television or sitting in a corner. She was active and alert so her special job was the shop at Marbridge ranch, a Texas-style cottage built on the campus for just a person like Bea. People brought second-hand goods of all kinds, which she priced and placed for sale.

When the thrift shop work was slow, Bea crossed the street and helped out in one of the twelve large greenhouses which Marbridge Ranch operated as a training and work station for the younger retarded men. Bea was very jealous of her job at the thrift shop. She believed that it was her responsibility alone — and she took that very seriously., Sometimes she would let a few others assist.

Robert McLaughlin, who broke his knee a few years ago at the ranch where he lived, was one of the best workers. He loved to mow the grass and was knowledgeable in watering and planting.

Even though Robert moved to the Villa, he went with the ranch men to the Marbridge hunting lease each fall; and more than likely, would return with a big buck.

Robert was against idleness. Since residing at the retirement home he has learned to fashion hook rugs. Beautiful examples of his work were hung about the walls of the retirement home. One of his most cherished pieces was a large hooked masterpiece featuring a deer with an expanse of antlers. It hung just outside his bedroom door.

Robert also could still sit on a dock and fish, and when possible went to Marbridge's fishing condo on the Gulf Coast at Rockport.

Robert's seniority at Marbridge made him one of the major "historians" of the whole operation.

On entering the Villa, a visitor was met by a loud "squawk!" That would be the cockateel which someone gave to the home and which so many of the residents would cuss. But they would not get rid of the loud bird for anything.

The visitor also realizes that "this doesn't even *smell* like a nursing home!" It smelled fresh and it looked like a gaily decorated, fun retirement home, for sure. If it was raining, men and women were busy walking up and down the halls — to get in their "walking mileage." Some were pushing others in wheelchairs.

On a large bulletin board in the hall, not far from the administrative offices, were pictures of "winged shoes" (sneakers) on which were the walkers' names in silver glitter. There were wings on every shoe and a sign above that says "Watch us Fly!" There was a silver star on shoes for each mile the "owner" walked. Most of the time the residents walked down Marbridge's shady paths — even as far as the stables.

Adjoining this bulletin board was the picture-board, with photos of the last special event at the villa — like the Mardi Gras celebration or the tour to LBJ Ranch.

Down another wing the residents had placed their names on their rooms. One door had a sign that said "Pauline's Room," and it was done in letters of rainbow colors, each letter decorated with flowers. On another door was a sign with a hand depicting a pointer finger. It said "Joe Brown's Room" this way.

Jose and David were laundrymen for the Villa, and residents themselves. David was originally in charge of this important work station, but when Jose came to the Villa, he attached himself to David and the laundry job. Jose did not speak English, but he and David managed the daily clean-clothes task. They would push the big carts of dirty laundry — or clean — up and down the halls all day long. Their job was important, and they knew it.

The men and women were encouraged to do whatever small jobs they could such as helping set the dining tables, wrapping silverware in the napkins and helping clear the tables after meals. Pfluger called some his "personality kids," which were the ones who did not like to do anything. However, most all of them liked the monthly trips to town, which were taken in a large Villa van. The residents were divided into four men's groups and two women's groups for going to special events. Pfluger said sometimes they went to a "decent movie."

Regularly they were taken to a nearby library where they could check out books. Several times during the week they viewed video movies, complete with popcorn and snacks. Volunteers came to give manicures, conduct Bible studies and assist in the craft room. A large sign in a game room said: "I'm A Dilla From The Villa — Marbridge."

Besides the craft and game rooms. There was a large living room with television and fireplace, a smaller "study" room, a gym with exercise bicycles, physical therapy room with more bicycles, hair dryers, a blue tile sauna and a place where nurses aides gave baths to the infirmed.

The individual rooms, accommodating two persons each and with private baths, were much larger and colorful than the usual rooms in a retirement/nursing home. Nearly everyone had his own personal television set and could bring in cherished items.

On a typical day at the Villa, residents would arise at 6:30 or 7:00 A.M. Nurse's aides assisted those unable to get up and dress by themselves. A lively breakfast would be served at 7:30 A.M. Each meal was tailored to the individual's need. Their likes and dislikes, as well as doctor's orders for food, were carefully tabulated on everyone's card. Cards and statistics on their food consumption were kept by the kitchen staff.

Staff and aides were so careful with diet that some diabetics were almost off insulin. "We control it by diet," explained Pfluger. A registered dietician would spend several hours a month going over the different menus and organizing the food ordering.

"We are very specific about eating habits," said Pfluger, then laughed, "for instance, Jose likes very large servings. We have coffee ready at 10:00 A.M. and 2:00 P.M. for those old-timers who find coffee so important in their lives," he added.

After breakfast, residents went to their special jobs or participated in numerous activities like painting, gardening in good weather, caring for their own belongings when able, playing billiards, doing yardwork. Letter-writing was important. Sometimes one of the activity directors or a volunteer assisted; and if the resident had no one with whom to correspond, someone tried to secure a pen pal for them. Walking was on the schedule constantly. A good walker could go as far as the greenhouses, or, stretching it, to the horse stables. Exercise was at the top of the list. Even the most severely handicapped needed exercise. Those in wheel chairs were given arm and leg work outs. Some of the exercise classes were called "sittercize."

Pfluger said that "we want all of them to do something."

The more active ones sometimes joined the men at the ranch in such activities as bowling, swimming, choir, chapel on Sunday afternoons, church in town, woodworking, and ceramics. Some of the old-timers joined the bicyclers, even if on a three-wheeler, and were active Boy Scout members.

You have never really "seen" or "felt" the emotional tug of patriotism until you have seen a fully-outfitted boy scout, who was a senior retarded citizen, happily and proudly enter a scout meeting on a walker.

Some Villa people would get on the big Marbridge bus and attend ice shows, ballgames rodeos, and concerts, and visit the ranch barbershop when necessary.

Marbridge had always seemed to find plenty of volunteers for their facilities from churches, colleges, civic groups or neighbors. The volunteer group for the Villa — called Villa-gers — numbered about twenty-eight. In addition, the Knights of Columbus would send as many as twenty persons when requested. Volunteers came in the daytime to help with letter-writing or birthday parties. But mostly volunteers came at night, conducting Bible studies, sing-a-longs, bingo,

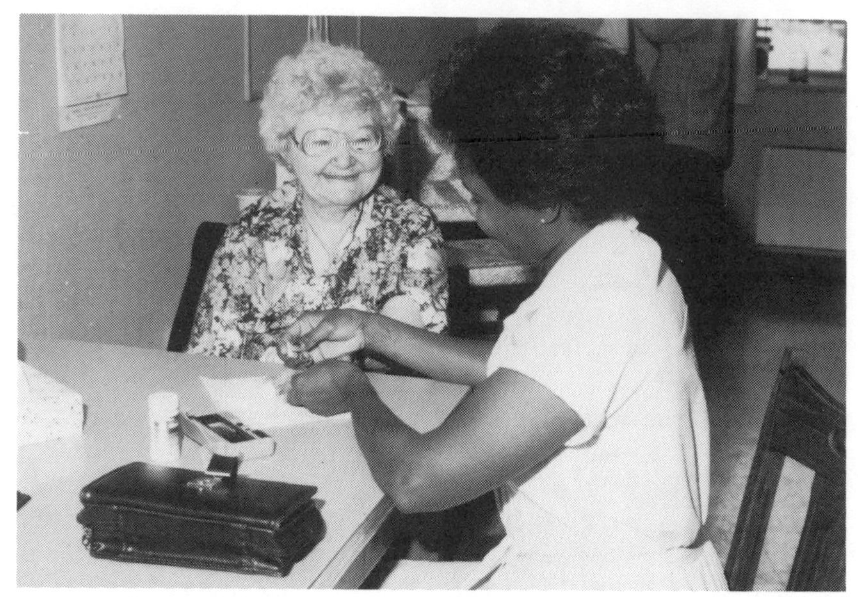

"Miss Sunshine" at the Villa is Adie Richard, left, with Mary Willie, a nurse's aide.

dramas, or dances. At one square dance exhibition, the residents began joining in — even David in his wheel chair, who was whirled around.

After evening activities, it was difficult to get some of the old-timers to bed. "They don't want to miss anything," said Pfluger. "We have to make them go to bed."

The Villa men and women seemed to have more visitors than the men at the ranch. "We could not keep them out, even if we wanted to," said Pfluger. Senior citizens, especially the retarded, loved animals, and the Villa had its share of dogs, cats and birds, including the noisy front-door parrot. Perhaps the favorite dog was "Sandy," that Pfluger found on a hunting trip. Sandy greeted all visitors and slept on a special chair in Pfluger's office.

Whenever possible, Villa residents entered the Special Olympics' Seniors Games. In 1987, twenty-eight participated, and the team came back with a first place trophy. In 1988, the Villa celebrated "nursing home week" May 9–13 in a big way. Colorful helium-filled balloons with fun messages floated into the sky while residents watched. Every resident received a special award for accomplishments, for walking, exercising, bowling, soaking up the sun and craft work.

A climax of the week was a beauty pageant at another retirement facility in Austin. Agnes Schwab, escorted by her brother Norbert Schwab, did a glamorous job in representing the Villa. Pfluger made it a point to deliver the Villa's daily mail. "This gives me an excuse to see them at least once a day." He also took his noon meal with them.

When the Marbridge Foundation realized the need for a retirement home and Mr. Bridges selected Pfluger as administrator, he had to get busy and prepare. While Mr. B with his remarkable ability to raise money, was collecting the $1,400,000 to build the Villa debt-free, Pfluger was enrolled in a part-time training course for nursing home administrators. This took about two years, then he worked one-half day in nursing homes until he received his official Texas nursing home administrator's license. By that time, the Villa was complete and ready for business.

One of Pfluger's greatest responsibilities was seeing that the Villa was always ready to pass inspection. State Nursing Home examiners never made appointments. Also, there were State Health Department requirements. That kept staffers on their toes at all times. Pfluger stressed such things as no "cross contamination" of clothing in the laundry process. To follow strict licensing guidelines, the Villa discontinued the use of bar soap and cloth towels. Only paper towels were in the residents' bathrooms; only soap dispensers were used.

"For our own protection," explained Pfluger, "We maintain strict discipline within the staff. There is endless paperwork, but all necessary. Everything is documented by the staff — aides, volunteers, nurses, all of us."

According to the Marbridge Foundation, the Villa remained at the top of every official requirement, but Pfluger insisted that his home go beyond that. "We want to do even better."

He said that most of the time, inspectors and health officials could not believe all the activities going on at the Villa. This retirement program operated from privately funded tuitions; Level III nursing care could be funded either privately or by Medicaid for those who qualified.

Pfluger believed there should be a Medicaid category for others besides Level III nursing — for those retarded senior citizens, like the ones who lived in the Villa.

"There was no funding for them when they were growing up, which left a void in their lives, and there still is a void in funds."

One reason the Villa's men and women were so happy, he be-

The Villa's resident leprechaun, Tommy Wood, doing a jig. You should see him in his Boy Scout uniform!

lieved was because, at last, someone was doing something special for them.

Mr. Bridges said there had never been any room at any Marbridge facility for anything but optimism. "We always have operated with a very positive attitude."

Days at the Villa were busy, as busy as each resident needed or wanted.

"We do have trouble — just like with any older citizen, but we know this. When you get older, there is a remarkable change in your behavior," explained Pfluger. "We all realize this, and we love them. The important thing is that they know we love them."

Pfluger hired all his employees. There was a licensed vocational nurse on twenty-four-hour duty and a registered nurse on call at all times. When necessary, a medical doctor or a social worker was called. He wanted his staff, as well as residents, to "never think old. That's why we all are here at the Villa today — to claim the gold."

In fact, most of the staff and volunteers, too, claimed that the residents "cheer us up — and even cheer up their visitors." The happy mood was catching, like in all Marbridge facilities. It was not downhill here — it was all *up*.

Kindness went right along with love and a sense of humor. On one occasion an aide heard Ronnie fussing about his feet hurting. As if it were all in a day's work, she said, "Well, Ronnie, you're wearing left shoes on both of your feet — and one shoe isn't yours. You need to put your name on them."

Millie Tootle, director of nursing, explained that the reason some of the retarded were at the Villa was that not only were they old, but they had physical and medical needs that a halfway house or other facility for the retarded did not offer. These residents needed closer watching by licensed medical personnel. Even some nursing homes did not have this.

She said "we have lots of diabetics, some with heart or lung conditions, some with seizures. We have to be able to give insulin and other shots. We must be able to draw blood and monitor medicine intakes.

The Villa had enough trained personnel, such as licensed nurses and aides, to carefully watch the special needs of all the senior citizens accepted at the Marbridge facility.

On one occasion the Villa accepted a woman who had come from another home, a home that admittedly could not handle her, "She misbehaved; wouldn't get out of bed," remembered Pfluger. We worked very hard with her; and once she began to cooperate, we bragged on her. She began to feel she had achieved a success. She does great now. The ol' boys and girls are just like all of us: they want to feel recognized for their accomplishments."

Admission criteria for the Villa were the same as for Marbridge's other facilities. Basically, the person had to be mentally retarded or brain damaged, have medical problems reviewed by doctor and nurse, not be emotionally disturbed or physically aggressive, and able to get around.

Senior citizens with vision and hearing losses were considered after review; persons supplied with Title 19 funding might be accepted with established level of care; and both men and women were accepted.

Residents understood when they arrived at the Villa that it became their true home. Many of them had spent their lives being shuffled about, uprooted time and again — and thus, were insecure. They realized at the Villa that their restless search for a better life had ended. These were days of reflection and spiritual reward as steps grew slower and energy level ebbed.

Here, in their declining golden years they came to know that they had found a home — at last!

— 14 —

Best Li'l Community Living House in Texas

"The main thing we try to give them here is the closest thing to a natural life as possible. All they need is a hand on their shoulder."

Latest dream of Ed and Marge Bridges became a reality in the middle of a thunder storm and a downpour of rain. At the dedication of Mabee Village at Manchaca nature had its way — but so did Marbridge Foundation. On November 8, 1987, Marbridge supporters and staff, new village residents and their parents gathered to dedicate the most unique living center in the world.

Mabee Village was somewhere between a place of security and a place of independence. It was somewhere between a modern condo development and a haven for the mentally handicapped. It was somewhere between the Bridges' dream and a growing necessity — the Marbridge Foundation's answer to halfway houses for the handicapped.

After thirty-five years down the road proving that the mentally retarded could be habilitated, Ed and Marge Bridges had done it again! The Plan was working!

W. B. Gildart, with no family of his own, had deeded the property on which Mabee stood to the Foundation when he died. He wouldn't be surprised that this latest dream had come true.

As next door neighbor to the ranch for many years, Gildart watched Marbridge grow. He loved the men and he appreciated what the Bridges were doing. He would have been proud to have been present at the dedication November 8, 1987. At the dedication, Mr. B said "this village of peace and contentment is a place where men and

Benny Howard, third from left, is administrator at Mabee Village. Residents with him are, left to right, Kurt Gaulke, Robert Bond, and James Ball.

women can communicate with nature. We try to give them the closest to a natural life as possible. All they need is a hand on their shoulder."

Rev. Jack Burton, pastor of Austin's Woodlawn Baptist Church and main speaker, said the village represented "living monuments erected by people of vision and faith today who believe in the value of human lives, despite handicaps and limitations."

Mrs. B (Mama B) said, "Now I guess I have a whole village to mother."

Mabee Administrator Benny Howard said "I feel we have the best facility in America. It's ultra modern, progressive, and revolutionary. Of course, I'm prejudiced, but we have the best group of residents and staff anywhere." In the near future, we will see Mabee Village assume a state-of-the-art image." Howard was right! A brief year later Mabee Village had a national reputation as an innovative, successful "state-of-the-art" model facility.

Within two weeks Howard began receiving calls from others in the halfway house business wanting to visit, look and discover. He said previously some state institutions had experimented in independent living status for some of their residents, allowing a few of them to live in a cottage behind the main buildings.

The program for Mabee, according to its administrator, was to teach residents independent living skills and also help them develop a trade which would enable them to hold jobs in communities and be able to compete in the job market.

"It's quite an adjustment to come here," he added, "especially if they have been in a family home or an institution."

There was a lot of transition to make; the program was fast-paced. Residents wanted to be as normal as possible, so Mabee Village presented a realistic setting, and the staff tried hard to get a new resident off on the right foot. Other residents contributed much toward helping a new person become acclimated. Each one was a support to the other. New ones saw what successes the older residents were having, so they could set goals for themselves — and be like their neighbor or housemate. In the interaction, Mabee residents became a team.

But at the first, the focus was on making the new ones feel at home and not be sad or lonely. Many times Howard or other staffers would ask an older resident to lend a hand. Most were happy to do so. Everyone wanted to be needed, the one giving and the one receiving.

In formulating the program and carrying on the objectives set by Marbridge Foundation, Howard said Mr. B asked him, mainly, "to make rational decisions." Howard had been working for Marbridge over seven years as administrator of the Austin Marbridge House. He felt he had learned Mr. and Mrs. B's thoughts regarding community living centers. He was aware that they wanted as many of the Marbridge people as possible to learn "to do it on their own."

The visitor to Mabee Village would enter an impressive gateway just off Texas ranchroad 1626, drive through the main grounds of Marbridge Ranch and wind through a couple of fields which were beginning to look like lawns or recreation fields. The fourteen ultra-modern, brick cottages had their own lawns and landscaping and resembled an average neighborhood or condominium complex.

In the center was an administration building with a kitchen and dining room and a separate large laundry room. The village was surrounded by trees; and near to Marbridge's famous Bear Creek, running cool and clean through the ranch.

The residents, all of whom were friendly, would wave to visitors and some were working in the yards or washing windows; others playing volleyball or practicing softball, and a group seated at a picnic table "shootin' the breeze." A dream had become a reality!

In addition, some residents came from Texas Rehabilitation Commission referrals; some came from Marbridge Ranch where they were trained; several entered directly from an institution.

In a way, said Howard, some were like bringing in a "piece of raw material which we must make functional." They each had abilities to be developed.

Many of the residents had a fairly high I.Q. for mentally retarded persons. Soon they would be able to take an apartment in town. This would be when they had learned how to take total care of themselves, personally and job-wise.

On the grounds of Mabee Village the residents had their own subculture. They formed social clicks just like everyone else, made their own friends and picked their own leaders. They created much of their activities and developed their own identities.

The leadership in creating the new Bridges dream was composed of Ed and Marge Bridges; Jack Wood, Dallas architect; the Howe Company General Contractors; Randolph Walker, Marbridge building administrator; Chris Winslow, landscape contractor and administrator of the Marbridge Greenhouses, and Benny Howard, administrator of the new facility. Each of these felt some of the dream was theirs.

The fourteen brick cottages, each housing eight residents, lined the inner, circling drive deeply shaded by giant oak trees. Mabee Village was just five minutes from the Marbridge Ranch and Foundation headquarters.

Of the fourteen cottages, three men and one woman's cottages were called "independent living" areas. Inside were a complete kitchen, washer and dryer, and larger rooms, so that, indeed, the residents were independent. They did not eat at the central dining room of the Village. It was the nearest to normal life for Mabee people. At some point, some of them would move on to living completely independently in nearby communities.

Mabee Village did not appear to be an institution for the mentally retarded. The residents — some one hundred and twelve when filled to capacity — were a cross-section of habilitated retardants, explained Howard. They were men and women of diverse backgrounds who found they could live in an independent-type environment, but with the security of supervision. They wanted to work for a living — and that was what the Village was all about.

Many of them had lived in the Dallas Marbridge House, which closed when Mabee Village came into being, or the Austin Marbridge

House, which for the past several years had been three ranch houses on the edge of Marbridge.

Mabee Village was a community living center operated by the Marbridge Foundation and similar to the ones in Houston and Abilene. Major differences were that it was co-educational and had an innovative construction concept.

Benny Howard's staff would tell you that the success of the Village had been due to his dedicated efforts, his foresight and his affable but firm leadership. He spoke knowledgeably, had the experience to back it up, and was a man of strength and security. He had the physical appearance of an offensive lineman for a pro football team.

Howard's degree from Sul Ross University at Alpine, had the double majors of sociology and physical education. He had been offered coaching positions from time to time during the past years, but said he "came to realize that working with the mentally retarded was where I wanted to be."

Before joining the Marbridge staff, Howard had a great deal of experience at the Austin State School, where he served in various capacities, including special education teacher, vocational teacher, supervisor of the workshop, and coordinator of the recreation program. He also had worked for the Travis State School and Longhorn School, both near Austin. These positions spanned the years 1972 to 1978 at which time he went into private business for two years. But his field was rehabilitation and he fit the Marbridge mold.

Where Mr. B was a master fund-raiser, Howard was a master recruiter. During the first year at Mabee Village, Howard traveled the state talking to counselors, social service agencies, decision-makers and sometimes parents. He wanted to keep the Village full; and when a resident moved on, he wanted one ready immediately to fill the vacancy.

He had a long list of referrals and applications "waiting" for approval. But he had to personally be assured that the prospective resident would fit into the Village program. This process was painstaking and certainly required experienced and thoughtful screening — plus good common sense. Howard called this "working a referral." He said that in his visit about the state he realized that he was representing the Marbridge Foundation as a whole. He did not have a "marketing strategy." He discovered that — like the ranch — he did not need one. Word-of-mouth preceded him, and most of those with whom he met already knew about the Marbridge Plan and had great respect for Mr. B.

In addition, he discovered that some of the counselors and agency personnel still remembered the early days of Marbridge and people like Ralph Pfluger and Randolph Walker, who helped promote the plan. During a visit with a counselor in Victoria, he met a regional director of the Texas Rehab Commission who once worked for Marbridge in Odessa. Howard had to closely budget his time in order to visit over the state and keep tabs on all Mabee activities, too.

It took a lot of man-hours. It took the same man-hours during the time he was "in on" all Mabee Village's development and construction and then moving Austin and Dallas residents to the new site.

Howard wanted to maintain a "proper balance" at Mabee Village and bringing together a homogenous group of 112 retarded persons was no easy task. Visits over the state paid off during the year, Howard believed. "The successes for just one short year were achieved because of good referrals," he explained. These were from all over the nation, although only about ten percent of Mabee's residents were from out of state. Inquiries from throughout the nation came in daily. Howard said he had at least two or three personal visits from out-of-state persons, mostly professionals, every week. To keep a properly balanced percentage from over Texas, Howard began concentrating on the Rio Grande Valley region.

Keeping the lines of referrals open was important to Howard and to Mabee Village. If a counselor in some part of Texas left, Howard paid a call on the new replacement as soon as possible.

Howard said that when he first walked into an office, "I first had to sell myself, then sell the facility." It might, also, have meant that he had to convince a parent that the money spent by them while their son or daughter was being made work-ready was money well spent. "It took a commitment that was sometimes difficult to make."

For proper presentation, laughed Howard, in West Texas "I wear my good western boots . . . but I have to be versatile." He was required to identify with the urban people one day, and rural the next. This took learning to "read people," and adjusting to the situation — to be convincing and recruit for Mabee. Sometimes he found himself also selling the ranch when he found a suitable prospect for its program.

Howard worked on a tight schedule, depending upon a small, but well qualified, staff. He hired a staffer the same as Marbridge

Ranch would — one that was versatile and could fill many posts and many needs. He hired one who could not be manipulated by the residents, one who would find himself totally involved in the lives of Mabee men and women and one that realized that forty hours a week was just the beginning.

Howard indicated he had taken note of the type of employee hired at Marbridge Ranch when he first came.

"I was most impressed, and it made me want to be able to fit that mold. You know, the type of staffer who will bring his own tools from home if necessary to get the job done."

"You can't get as much out of an individual if his work is so classified, so I looked for people with adaptable skills." This was one reason Mabee Village could claim so much success.

Gary Noonan, a masters degree education major from the University of Oklahoma, had been with Marbridge Ranch eight years. He was under sponsorship of the Austin Independent School District as a vocational adjustment coordinator.

Since Mabee opened, Noonan had spent one-half day in the ranch classroom then he devoted the remainder of his time to the some seventeen Mabee men and women under twenty-two years old who were eligible for classroom special education. He also assisted Ms. Burdett in job placement.

However, Noonan was as versatile as the other staffers, and could be seen about the Marbridge acreage, ranging from the Village to the ranch to the greenhouses, checking on his students.

Noonan, said he strived to teach the residents functional words that could be used in the community. He taught each of his students in a different way. Noonan liked his Job, and the uniqueness of all Marbridge facilities.

"It's amazing how the greenhouses have grown in the eight years I've been here. Then there is the extended care at the retirement Villa, where a person can spend his whole life here."

Noonan liked such things as the hunting and fishing opportunities for a Marbridge resident. This highly qualified teacher always showed how much he cared for his students and other residents. Like most of the staff, he had been at Marbridge long enough to know everyone.

Mabee Village was different from other halfway houses across the nation because there was more "going on" at this community living center.

Arthur Harrison might be called "the official greeter" at Mabee Village. He is usually out front somewhere, waving to all those coming and going.

Residents who were not out on jobs at any given moment were involved in chores about the Village or participating in recreational activities, some planned and some of their own making.

During the day, there were usually continuous volleyball games, softball practice, cards and other games in the dining hall, which doubled as the recreation room. Among chores, for which they are paid, were helping in the kitchen, washing windows, watering lawns and plants, keeping the administration office clean, and other tasks. Each cottage had to be kept in order at all times by the ones living there. If Mabee homes and grounds were not impeccable, Howard wanted to know the reason why. Under "recreation" were parties. A group of volunteers would have monthly celebrations for birthdays and help get everything ready for holidays. Each resident would receive a birthday cake and gift.

Shopping trips to town were planned on a regular basis. Parties and other activities for all the Central Texas halfway houses were offered by the Travis County Mental Health/Mental Retardation organization and the Parks and Recreation Department of Austin. Not a week went by without a party or dance of some sort. Travis County MH/MR had a popular weekly "canteen" with dancing, games and fun.

Many times Mabee residents got together with residents of the Mary Lee School, which came into being after Marbridge's founding and was patterned after the Marbridge Plan. On a typical night, a dozen or more residents would be transported to the canteen, a bunch going bowling, some attending a movie in town, others watching television in their own cottage. Some of the residents were allowed personal freedom in off-hours when they could visit friends off campus. However, a complete schedule was carefully kept on residents so that the staff knew where they were at all times — and with whom. Residents were not allowed their own car. Men and women could not visit in each other's cottages.

Recreation, also, was scheduled in as normal a setting as possible. For instance, residents would rather go into Austin to swim instead of going to the ranch pool. They went their own way for bowling, church and many other activities into the normal community area. They also planned their own vacations.

They learned a great deal about community and city activities — like who was running for Austin mayor or councilman and what was going to be done with the old airport. Debates over local, state, and national issues were heard often at Mabee Village. Howard said that going co-educational had not brought any real problems. Everyone seemed to adjust and follow rules and guidelines. Being co-educational was like "the normal world," so it performed a much needed function for the retarded men and women. This in itself was a training device. That was perhaps the major reason for being co-educational.

Mabee's PSA (personal social adjustment) class was held each evening, Monday through Friday, from 7:00 to 8:30 P.M. Especially at the beginning of a resident's life in Mabee Village these classes were extremely important. At first many did not know how to respond to the other sex. They did not know how to interact. But they soon learned. As yet there had been no romances blooming on the Mabee campus.

The staff had found that in the co-educational setting girls did indeed, argue more than the men. This was a little problem they faced, as well as the problem that all the residents would compete for attention. There was some friction, according to Howard — but, again, this was certainly normal. The normal around Mabee was that "nobody sits around doing nothing." Marbridge philosophy, of course was "keep them busy; keep them happy."

Rick Thorpe, Mabee resident, produced a monthly newspaper *The Village.* "He was the nosiest one here," explained Burdett, "so we just made him the newspaperman." Thorpe's newsletter covered stories of new residents, new jobs, jokes, trips, recreation events, and poems by residents.

Since the population of the Village was becoming stabilized, Howard began working on the training program.

"We are effective in job placement. We will also have a top program of training services to continue our effective image."

"My goal is to have ninety to ninety-five percent employed most of the time."

If a state agency payed the tuition for a resident, Marbridge followed the training directions which the agency suggested. However, like at all Marbridge facilities, Howard wanted to direct the program as much as possible.

Some residents were sent to certified sheltered workshops for specific training after he determined what their special skills were or could become. Among such operations were Vocational, Inc., and the Goodwill Industries. Goodwill also offered some of the residents contract work.

By far, the employer that had hired the most Marbridge workers, was Barton Creek Country Club and Convention Center west of Austin in the suburb of Westlake Hills. At one time nineteen Mabee residents were employed in their laundry rooms, kitchens and housekeeping department. Three shifts of vans delivered the Marbridge residents to work.

Major selling points to a prospective employer were — "People available for work with experience or training; and available transportation." At least the employer knew that Mabee would see to it that the worker was delivered — and on time. They also knew that the Mabee staff was available if any problems arose.

There was pride in all the residents of Mabee Village; and a lot of peer pressure which kept them striving to excel.

Freddy Mitchell was born to a retarded mother in a state hospital. He became a resident of the Austin facility twenty years ago, and had worked successfully at the Barton Creek Country Club for eighteen of those years. He had missed few days of work. One time he went to work so ill, the manager called Marbridge to come after him. He was generally known at Barton Creek Club as "the best pots-and-pans man" they had.

Judy Burdett, left, job placement counselor, with residents, Alice Papadakis, center, and Cletus Johnson.

Steve Stovall was one of the best liked residents of Mabee Village. He had been with the Austin Marbridge facility since 1968 and had worked very productively at the Texas Purchasing and General Services Division for nine years. His hobby was cooking and Steve filled in as a relief cook on weekends for the ranch. During his years with Marbridge other residents had considered him a leader, an achiever, and an inspiration to others.

Reymundo Garza, age thirty-eight, was a longtime employee of The University of Texas where he liked to work out in a gym with co-workers. He maximized the use of the Austin public transportation system and frequently made town trips all on his own. He, too, set a good example for his co-residents at Mabee. Another achiever was John Haines who last year was named "Worker of the Year" by Goodwill Industries, Inc.

Not long ago Oscar Robinson, who had been with this country club and in the Austin house since 1974, was able to move into his own apartment, assuming full control of his work and his life. He fulfilled Marbridge's dream for their men. A full-time Villa employee, who until last year was, first at the ranch for special training, and then at the Dallas, Houston and Austin houses, had a special romantic story.

Terry Darwin was married to Betty Sonic in August 1987, and they moved into an apartment in Austin. They were living and working — a normal couple in a normal community. However, in one way Terry was not quite at normal level, as he still received assistance from the Marbridge staff in the areas of money management, transportation assistance, and personal counseling. They were happy, tax-paying, wage-earning people making a "go" of it under special difficulties.

Hope, Howard's assistant said she was "proud to work at Mabee Village." When hired she said Mr. B told her he wanted her "to be a good mother to the residents and see that their needs are met."

During her time there, Hope had seen many of them learning how to care for themselves and make decisions on their own.

She explained how their personal lives were concerns of all the staff. They understood what it meant to come back from the normal community and have a "hurt" inside. The staff dealt with this and helped them over the hurts and humps. They all tried very hard. They were succeeding to a degree not thought possible just a few years before.

Mabee Village was the center of a heart-warming story in mid-1988. One day a resident, Alton Babin, went into the office and asked the secretary to give him the telephone number of his sister. Alton had been taken from his family in Louisiana when he was five years old and placed in various state homes and institutions by that state's Health and Human Resources Department. Rose Marie, a sister, who had once lived in Lafayette, Louisiana, was located.

She was overwhelmed and happy to hear from her little brother, now aged thirty-three, who she thought had been lost forever. Alton took a vacation and visited her. Then he came back to pack, with the good news that she wanted him to come live with her. He ended a twelve-year Marbridge residency reluctant, but happy.

A special success story for a Mabee man concerned William Hale, who moved there from the Dallas House where he worked for Furr's Cafeteria and was named an "employee of the month." He was an expert dishwasher — which led him to a job at one of Furr's Cafeterias in Austin a year ago. Later his employer moved him up to supervisor of all dishwashing. This promotion was because of his ability to monitor the washers and save perhaps one to one and a half hours of time each day. Becoming a supervisor was a "first" for Marbridge community living centers and maybe all such halfway houses, as William had been given supervisory authority over normal employees at the cafeteria.

Needless to say, everyone at Marbridge was very proud of William, who took pride in his work and achievement.

Each Mabee Cottage featured modern architectural lines, interestingly shaped windows, different exterior colors. Each was named for a person who had contributed toward the success of the Marbridge Plan. Two were named for incorporators who were members of the first board, H. M. Totland and Dr. Carlyle Marney. Another was named for Matthew Van Winkle, a member of the first board.

The three served on the Foundation board for many terms. The name of another former board member, Dr. R. O. (Sam) Swearingen, appeared on a cottage. He was Marbridge's first doctor.

Two cottages were named in honor of two longtime board members W. L. Todd and Gregg Ring, who were also generous contributors who had sons at Marbridge ranch.

The name of Theo Davis, a loyal supporter, was on a cottage. Marbridge was recipient of funds under Theo P. Davis charity trust.

Others with sons at Marbridge Ranch who had been generous supporters of the Foundation for whom cottages were named included J. W. Lawless and Jim Taylor, Mr. and Mrs. W. H. Kirk, Mr. and Mrs. John Justin, and Mrs. Esther Carney.

W. B. Gildart donated the land on which the Village was built. One of the independent living houses was named for Mama B., incorporator, board member since Marbridge's inception and former housemother, cook, nurse, and counselor for the ranch. The Mabee Village was named in honor of the J. E. and L. E. Mabee Foundation of Tulsa, which helped fund both the Village and the retirement Villa. Mama B said it took four years of planning and two years of fund-raising to build the $1.6 million community living center.

"Every one of the parents gave something," said Mr. B, "which showed that they wanted it, too."

He pointed out that the Marbridge Foundation had been supplying retarded men and women to satisfied employers for decades in Houston, Dallas, Abilene, and Austin.

"The new state-approved Mabee Village will provide a home-away-from-home for one hundred and twelve men and women who are going to be meeting Austin's needs for dependable workers for many years to come," he declared, adding "as we review each year of progress of Marbridge, we can see that things have happened. Things that are exciting, things that are helpful, things that make us thankful to God that we can have progress and a part in shaping productive lives."

— 15 —

No Stopping Now! On To The Moon!

"We have learned not to limit what God can do."

June 3, 1982

A large crowd at the plush Sheraton Hotel in Boston rose to a standing ovation as Ed and Marge Bridges were presented a special award for their work as pioneers in habilitation of the mentally retarded. It was the 101st annual convention of the American Association on Mental Deficiency. This was the ultimate honor among many others they had received during the twenty-nine-year history of the Marbridge Plan which they conceived, developed and expanded in Texas. Symbolically, it was the climax of a dream originating with the necessity to create a suitable, loving and secure home for their brain-damaged son, Jim. In founding this home on Marbridge Ranch, they helped hundreds of other Jims and their families, bringing them out of the darkness of despair and setting them on the road to happy lives.

The Association called them "pioneers" in the habilitation field. Pioneering became a specialty to this couple who long ago said, "No, we will not place our son in an institution where he will be fed and clothed and set in a corner." Deep inside they had an unwavering idea that some brain-damaged and some mentally retarded persons could be taught a skill that would bring happiness and a sense of worth to them. Ed and Marge Bridges were right.

Their pioneering idea blossomed and succeeded, in spite of the pessimistic words of doctors, psychologists and psychiatrists. It was not too many years into the Plan that these same professionals" came to

Marbridge Ranch to observe and find out how they achieved the "impossible dream."

Twenty-seven years had sped by at Marbridge Ranch, and in 1988 other pioneering ideas of Marge and Ed Bridges had come to pass and established the determined couple as authorities, by trial-and-error experience, in the habilitation of the retarded. They pioneered the idea of setting up halfway houses for the retarded, which they called community living centers, for men and women they trained to hold jobs in normal communities. These were located across Texas and were generally considered prototype facilities. They pioneered the idea of a retirement/nursing home for retarded senior citizens. Their retirement Villa on Marbridge Ranch was generally considered "the showplace" of such homes.

When the Bridges decided to found Marbridge as a non-profit corporation, they decided also that the only thing to do was to pay their own way — just like all other supporters of the Foundation. Since the very first month, the tuition for their son, Jim, was paid on time and in the same amount as all other residents' tuitions.

However, where they were singularly different from everyone else was that they already had in their will a major clause that deeded all properties owned by them and gave all money left upon their deaths to Marbridge. Until Jim's death, he would be cared for at Marbridge under a trust. The Marbridge Plan achieved every result desired; Ed and Marge's plan had worked!

It continued to work, for as long as there were the Bridges, there would be dreams of more programs to come for the mentally retarded. And when there were no longer a Marge or an Ed Bridges, the Marbridge concept would continue in perpetuity for all the Jims-to-come.

Meanwhile, back to 1982, Marbridge not only received top national honors for the two founders, but acquired a new, modern greenhouse number five for the ranch. Increasing demand and expanding interest in the Marbridge nursery made the new building imperative.

In this year, the special education classroom, which included a woodworking shop, metal shop and ceramics studio, was destroyed by fire. The mat-making, welding and metal work stations were discontinued because not enough men were interested in these as in similar crafts. Here again, Marbridge left no stone unturned in exploring suitable work for the men to learn.

By the fall of 1982, special education classes had reopened in a

Ralph Pfluger, vice-president of the Foundation, former business manager and now administrator of the Marbridge Villa, has been a key figure in the Foundation's growth over the years.

new location on the campus. The original greenhouse was converted into a modern classroom.

Other progressive steps included:

* Expansion of the Foundation's administrative building to consolidate all business offices and install a battery of computers.

* Friends of Mr. B gave him a surprise seventy-fifth birthday party in September, complete with Santa Claus and Christmas tree.

* Greenhouse number six went up in September.

* Budget review in October disclosed that the Marbridge Foundation had become a non-profit $4,000,000 enterprise.

* Greenhouse number seven was installed in horticulture area in November.

* The Oak Leaves volunteer group netted $6,500 from a garage sale.

Over 400 persons attended the Villa's dedication in April 1982 from all over the nation. Keynote speakers were Dr. Browning Ware, pastor of Austin's First Baptist Church, and Dr. Darrell Mase, retired dean of the College of Health Related Professions, University of Florida.

To close out 1983, Marbridge decided to discontinue making mesquite clocks, and another fire destroyed the office, records, and equipment of the horticulture center. Most nursery stock was undamaged.

The greenhouse business kept booming, and greenhouse number eight went up. Winslow and the men who worked with him or were in training were busy, morning to night — almost seven days a week.

An emotional highlight of the year was a ceremony at the Christmas party honoring residents of Marbridge Ranch who had been there ten years or more. Fifty-three men proudly accepted certificates, a number having been residents for almost all the twenty-eight years. Not to be outdone by the ranch men, the Villa gardeners took charge of a new greenhouse number nine built in 1985. But greenhouse number ten also was completed that year in the horticultural area to provide for expansion of services to the public.

Marbridge Villa completed its second year of operation with all but seven of the fifty-two beds occupied. The Marbridge Plan was working!

Another sixteen men received their ten-year certificates at the 32nd annual anniversary barbecue in Todd Amphitheatre on the campus. By far the biggest celebration in 1985 was dedication of the Chapel of Love. On the outside of the 200-seat chapel, which enhanced the entrance to the ranch, was not only the name but the words, *all faiths."*

On Sunday mornings residents were transported to churches or on Fridays to synagogues of their choice, but each Sunday afternoon at two o'clock, men and women from the ranch and Villa gathered in their own chapel for an all-faiths worship service. The public was always welcomed, and various neighboring churches took turns conducting the services.

The chapel was a dream of Mama Bridges and Randolph Walker, who both thought the men needed their own place of worship. Marbridge residents enjoyed going to church in town, but they knew they were different, and Mama B and Walker envisioned a chapel on the Ranch especially for them where no congregation would unintentionally treat them differently. They talked for years, until Mr. B got a fund drive going and the idea blossomed into reality.

Architect Jack Wood, who had served the Foundation as a board member, designed the stained glass windows. They depicted in glorious color familiar Bible stories. On one side were scenes from the story of Noah and the ark, the building of the ark, the animals two-by-two, the rain and flood, and finally God's rainbow of promise.

On the other wall were windows telling of the flight of Joseph and Mary into Egypt, Jesus and the little children of the world, Christ feeding the 5,000, Jesus on the cross, and finally Jesus ascending into Heaven.

During a service, visitors would note the happy faces of the ranch worshipers, and their pride as their own special choir marched slowly down the red-carpeted aisle. They were elegant in deep orange colored robes with brown satin collars. Some with walking problems might hobble a bit, favoring one leg and a man held his head to one side awkwardly. Some seemed a bit confused and hesitant but the ones in back would give them a little nudge.

There was nothing hesitant about their enthusiasm for song — the language of the angels. What mattered if off-key, what mattered if only a mumbling or a humming, what mattered if no song at all but a tambourine to accompany the rest of the men. They would try very hard, were proud of themselves, and loved the choir, and their own chapel.

For . . . "even as ye have done it unto the least of these, ye have done it unto me . . ."

The Chapel of Love was the first building seen upon entering the ranch's two gates, each flanked by brick columns.

It rested securely between a neatly rowed field of vegetables and a lawn sprinkled by wild flowers. Constructed of soft brown brick, a slim copper-clad spire hovered above the roof and was topped by a narrow cross.

The belfry chimed out lovely music over the gardens and stables and dormitories daily promptly at 7:00 A.M., 11:45 A.M. and 4:45 P.M., just before meals. Religious music with which the residents were familiar was played by programmable tapes. At special seasons, like Christmas, appropriate music was played. The system was set up so that Marbridge could "tailor-make" the chimed music to the likes and listening pleasure of the men and women.

The entrance to the chapel was enhanced by a square pool whose waters rippled under a tiered waterfall. Worshipers entered through carved wooden double doors. The hall featured handpainted wooden wall hangings, and the pews had red velvet pillows to match the red carpeting. Floors were of parquet and walls of redwood.

A piano, organ, choir loft, pulpit and communion table faced another stained glass window, raising from the floor to meet the ceiling. At about 2:00 P.M. when the sun was shining on Sunday afternoons, the array of colors filtering through the multi-colored, rectangular stained glass pieces, did, indeed, seem to be coming straight from Heaven, specially sent for God's special men.

Once more, in 1986, one of the big barns full of hay burned. No causes for the destruction of the two hay barns and the greenhouse offices and records have ever been determined. The good news in 1986 was the gift of four miniature horses from South Carolina by Mr. B and Mama B. Notwithstanding the fact that this couple donated their lives to Marbridge, they were known frequently to donate other things as private citizens — money, merchandise, products, horses, usually whatever was needed.

Ranch mascots were a miniature stallion named Mr. Ed, and three fillies, Miss Marge, Della, and Tera.

Construction during 1986 included two new greenhouses, number eleven and twelve; and an impressive new entrance driveway to the ranch campus. This was necessary when Travis County moved Bliss Spillar Lane in front of the ranch several hundred feet south and widened it to four lanes. The old road became an inner-campus drive for Marbridge only.

This brought the fields owned by Marbridge, which were once across the road, onto the main campus. Thus when you drove through the pillars there were fields of wild flowers or crops growing on each side.

The year 1986 was marked by the phasing-out of all beef cattle, chickens and egg production. General farming and raising of livestock ended. The only livestock remaining were ten riding horses, four miniature horses, and two or three hogs. Fruit orchards and hay fields remained productive, and horticulture, including a small vegetable garden area.

Another honor came to Ed Bridges in early 1987. He was named one of the "Ten Outstanding Citizens of Austin" by the Austin Pastoral Counseling Service for his lifelong contribution to the care and habilitation of mentally retarded adults.

He also celebrated his eightieth birthday at a party given by friends. Typically, his response to a speech by administrator Pfluger was a "sincere thanks" and then he gave the caterer a boost by recommending him to all present.

It took almost a year for construction of the Marbridge Foundation's "crowning glory" of their community living centers. The inno-

Part of vacation fun for Marbridge men and women is a trip to the Foundation's fishing condo on the Texas Gulf Coast at Rockport.

vative and remarkably beautiful Mabee Village opened in October and was dedicated in November.

The new Respite Care Program was opened for mentally retarded males, age fifteen and over, who were given respite admission for any period of time — three days to three months. It was designed as an aid for families who needed a little rest from care of such a son and also as an introduction for him to the learning program at Marbridge Ranch. According to Dr. Peck, this program worked quite well.

Another opening was billed as "the grand opening" of the Marbridge Thrift Shop for sale of surplus clothing and other articles donated to the ranch. The first woman admitted to the Villa — Bea Stone — was placed in charge of the shop. The ranch and all its satelites were going strong at the beginning of 1988 — there was no stopping now!

The Marbridge Plan continued as a model habilitation concept. In the past it had served as a definite influence for similar operations — like the Mary Lee School headquartered in Austin which was patterned after the Marbridge concept.

No doubt about it, the fame Marbridge had received for its thirty-five years had spread to the far corners of the nation — and to some corners of the world. The Bridges were happy about this because there seemed to be a continuous need for centers of learning and living for all types of handicapped persons.

Among those who would sing the praises of Marbridge was Dr. William Fraenkel, a consultant on vocational habilitation for the National Association for Retarded Citizens.

One time Hogg Foundation paid the expenses of Mr. Bridges to go to Oklahoma and consult with O'Neal Netherland and others interested in upgrading a center for the retarded named McCall Chapel. Mr. B spent two days with the leaders of McCall Chapel.

It was several years before he again heard from Netherland, who, coincidentally, had followed in the footsteps of Mr. B. He resigned as executive vice president of a large bank in Tulsa, Oklahoma, and took over this school, developing it into a successful operation similar to Marbridge. Netherland told Mr. B that it was his consultation which set the Oklahoma group "on the right track."

About 1965, Mr. B had a visit from Mr. and Mrs. Jimmy Green of Waxhaw, North Carolina, who had heard of Marbridge Ranch and its successful programs. They spent several days going over the entire operation very thoroughly and questioning Mr. B for long hours. Early in 1988 — twenty-three years later — Mr. B had a call from Green. He talked almost an hour, telling him of his facility in North Carolina patterned after Marbridge. He was very enthusiastic about his success and said he now had over 400 retarded and other handicapped persons enrolled in his facility.

"I can never forget you," he told the Marbridge founder. The Marbridge Plan was working!

Evergreen was a successful habilitation operation in Freeport, Louisiana. But many years ago, like the men from North Carolina and Oklahoma, the directors of Evergreen consulted with the administrators of Marbridge. They returned several more times, studying the Marbridge Plan and making notes of all the programs, rules and regulations. This was just one of numerous facilities that received good groundwork from Marbridge.

After a recent visit with the Bridges, brother Paul of North Carolina, had this to say in a letter:

> I met and talked with the men; felt the love and happiness they share. They look forward for each event planned for them. They have a gym, indoor swimming, picnic park, horseback riding, trips to Austin and many, many more activities.

"The men attend church on Sunday morning and the Chapel of Love at the ranch on Sunday afternoon. One would have to attend a service at the Chapel to know how much it means to the men. You would also have to meet the staff, and see them work with the men to know how dedicated they are to the ranch.

"It was wonderful to see the love and respect they have for Mr. and Mrs. J. E. Bridges, who I am very proud to say are my brother and sister-in-law."

In the thirty-five-year history of the Plan, there had only been sixteen persons to serve on the board of directors. Several of them had family members who were retarded; others were interested in the Plan and like most Marbridge supporters, stayed to help.

Incorporators who had been on the board continuously were of course J. E. and Marjorie Bridges, and Austin Banker Howard T. Cox.

Other original incorporators and longtime board members from Austin who were deceased, included Dr. Carlyle Marney, minister; John H. Winters, longtime director of the Texas Department of Public Welfare; H. M. Totland, businessman; and M. VanWinkle, UT professor of chemical engineering.

Others who served in the past were Pat Davis, Austin businessman; the late James Lawless, Austin contractor; and the late Dr. R. O. (Sam) Swearingen, Austin physician.

In addition to Mr. and Mrs. B and Cox, board members in 1988 included Jack Wood, Dallas architect; W. L. Todd, Dallas, independent oil producer; Gregg Ring, Houston manufacturer; Robert Jameson, Houston financier, E. Joe Duckworth, Austin investment attorney; Ralph Pfluger, administrator of the Villa; and Dr. John R. Peck, Marbridge psychologist-consultant.

Volunteers were the key to lots of fun for the men and women of all Marbridge facilities. The community living centers had less volunteer activities than the ranch and the Villa because the CLC men and women were in the normal stream of activity and could plan most of their own recreation and fun.

However, the ranch and the Villa were somewhat "homebound," so here was where the light of volunteers shone through.

In 1988 sixteen dedicated women formed the Oak Leaves group which planned a wide variety of programs for the ranch men. At the Villa were over twenty-nine members of the Vill-agers who came around regularly with fun ideas.

All the volunteers donated many hours of work and labor, per-

A lively group of volunters pictured at a Halloween party at the ranch, from left are Jessie B. Anderson, Agnes Guthrie, and Ruby Townsend.

sonal funds and ideas — and themselves — to this job which brought joy to the hearts of Marbridge residents.

For instance, each month the Oak Leaves gave a party at the Senior Dorm for all residents with birthdays that month. The two groups also decorated bulletin boards, provided refreshments for special parties at Christmas, Valentine, Halloween, and other holidays, helped decorate the dorms for all seasons, took residents on Easter egg hunts; helped them wrap presents or write letters or sew labels in clothing, arranged special entertainment at certain parties, and brought Christmas gifts.

The first volunteer at Marbridge who did all the above all by herself, plus lots of other duties, was Mama B, but soon she involved Mrs. W. H. Kirk and friends, fellow bridge club members and women of the First Baptist Church.

Among those first volunteers, and the first editor of the Marbridge quarterly newsletter was Wilma Jones, who said the reason the women gathered as volunteers for the ranch was that they all "felt the Plan was so important and so needed, and we wanted the men to have plenty of good times."

They called themselves "The Oak Leaves." This was the symbol of Marbridge itself and was originally drawn by Clarence Seagert, owner of an Austin direct mail advertising firm who became interested in the Plan. The board accepted the oak leaf as its permanent, official symbol.

Mr. B thought it was fitting because traditionally the oak tree was considered a symbol of strength and there were many beautiful oaks spread all over the 440 acres of the ranch. Under a reorganization plan Mrs. Ruby Townsend was the founding president of a new volunteer organization, also called the Oak Leaves. In addition to planning parties and generally bringing color and fun to the ranch, the Oak Leaves annually did their part to raise funds for use of the non-profit foundation.

In addition, the women donated money for arts and crafts supplies, video rentals, game tickets for men not able to buy them, magazines and books, and furniture and room accessories when needed. They also maintained a permanent Oak Leaves Benefit Fund under which they seek direct funds from the public. The Vill-agers assisted senior citizens with parties, decorations and special classes and programs and helped take them to appointments in town. Hardly a day passed without some Vill-agers in the midst of things at the Villa, even if it was just visiting.

Both volunteer groups were coordinated by Marbridge staffers to keep schedules moving smoothly. For the two dorms, Ed and Marge Bridges served as coordinators to the Oak Leaves, and vice president Williamson was staff advisor. The activity director served in this capacity at the Villa.

The very important volunteer arm at Marbridge Ranch had the objectives of helping the staff create homelike atmospheres, give personal attention and friendship to the residents and serve as a public relations laison between Marbridge and Austin.

Far too numerous and varied are the hundreds of donors to Marbridge over the years. It had received everything from food and clothes to windmills and eighteen-wheeler trucks. Marbridge found a use for anything.

Every donation, no matter how small, was recognized by letter and by publication in *The Experience* newsletter. Sometimes Mr. B publicly thanked donors at special ceremonies. But the founding couple never let a gift to their creation go without appreciation and proper recognition.

Special funds set up for Marbridge donors include Memorial,

Scholarship, and Building and other funds honored specific persons or residents. There was also a separate "contribution-in-kind" fund.

Donors ranged from personal and corporate to foundations and clubs. Even such agencies as the Texas Parks and Wildlife department had been among contributors. This agency for many years donated venison through deer killed by accident or confiscated by the game wardens.

Fund-raisers had been almost as varied as the donors and gifts. One time Mr. B produced "The Hank Snow Grand Ole Opry Show" featuring such well known western stars as Buck Owens, George Jones, Webb Pierce, and Hank Snow. Appeals through Mr. Bridges' column in *The Experience* always brought good results. Sometimes he would ask family members and friends who received *The Marbridge Experience* to help promote Marbridge:

> "Word of mouth is the bread and wine of our very existence . . . We need a continuous supply of young men from your communities to fill out our training programs at Marbridge. Please help us find those deserving young men in your town and get them to a place in the sun! We exist for their sake and like the U.S. Marines, all we need are a few good men!

. . . "and all they need is a hand on their shoulder."

— 16 —

Goodbye to Marbridge

"Mr. B has kept us in step all these years. He kept me sharp, I know, and Mr. B was always right on the track."

— *Randolph Walker*
Ranch Administrator

Dear Readers, the end of this book has come.

It is with sadness this writer is concluding her sojourn at Marbridge Ranch for I, too, have caught the "fever." I already know it is going to be difficult leaving these very special men.

I will feel that something is lacking every morning when I am not looking out of a temporary office on the ranch and seeing Mr. B make his stately way to the Senior Dorm to say good morning to his son. "How was the night, Jim?"

On the way he may pass David Justin, who is hurrying to feed his horses and dogs, or Bud Kirk, who is hurrying somewhere. I do not understand all Bud says, and he knows it. He talks and smiles anyway. However, Mr. B can understand everything Bud says. But then, Bud has been at Marbridge almost since its founding.

Now I won't be seeing Brian Ring anymore, coming in and out of the offices and carefully driving to and from errands in a ranch truck. Everyone is very proud of Brian's ability to accept responsible jobs, even off campus.

Mark Newsom won't be bringing me any more delicate yellow roses from the greenhouse for my desk, as he comes to empty trash baskets.

Jody Kahn won't be yelling to me across the lawns to come spend Saturday night in Winters Dorm with them. One time at a picnic Jody said, "I knew I'd help you finish that book."

And John Levitt won't be explaining city politics. Mike Pennington, standing so tall and proper, won't be asking me to sit at his table during lunch.

I won't be eating anymore at the other dorm, either, where Warren Todd worriedly explains another reason why everyone loves Texas more than San Francisco; and Jim Bridges, so gentlemanly, won't be telling me the entire schedule for a recent ice show the men attended.

Never again will Pat Galbreath offer to adopt me — that is, after Coach Coulter adopts him. Tom Raycraft will have to learn to put his own ribbons on his aged portable typewriter. Charles Puckett will continue handling his family's newsletter and reunions, and Gary Young, Robert Reed, Sloan McCalla, Gary Baker, and Pat Holcomb will all, breathlessly, continue their baseball talk. They have ribbons and trophies proving how well they have done on the diamond.

How nice it would be for me to have Bill Carney and Paul Stopford, two strong men of the ranch, at my home to help with all the heavy work.

I think until I go to that Great Beyond I will faintly hear Mark Wilson calling me "Mama" insisting I come to his room to see his computer. He writes mystery stories on it. Every story begins excitedly with: "It happened one cold rainy night as I was driving along . . ."

Steve Schlueter will continue being a loner and working hard in the outdoors. He is the silent type, for sure, but may manage a nice smile for you from his handsome face. Long will I see Leo Kuritza's funny impressions — of movie stars, TV stars and the ranch staff. Leo is one of the lovable Downs Syndrome men.

I suppose Bubba Sellers will always be slipping in the back door of the administration building to see his favorite people, the secretary Mary Gail Leming, and vice president Bob Williamson. The men have strict orders not to come to the offices uncalled, as they take too much time away from staff work. But they will continue to try.

Travis Pearson will nervously twist his hands, asking you where they are going to celebrate his birthday, will there be a cake and who is going to help him get dressed. Travis was twenty-five years old on May 13, 1988.

Everyone tells Nick Mainer to "open your eyes," as he tends to

Resident Steve Schlueter trims vines in Senior Dorm patio. Every resident of Marbridge gets paid for the work he does.

keep his eyes squinted as much as possible. This does not prevent him from telling you all about his girlfriend back home.

I shall be reminded of Jimmy Newland every time I see the wind spinning my wooden whirl-a-gig I tied from a tree in the front yard. A resident of the Villa, he said he didn't have a mother, so he made it for me.

Bobby Sheeks will always laugh when they kid him about getting out and going to the beer joint. He never denies it. I don't think any achievement by any man, henceforth, will tug at my heart as much as the first time I saw Willie Faloon, a Downs Syndrome man, dive into the ranch's big, clear pool. He came right back up and swam and played in the water like a happy little porpoise.

I shall never see again such comical jigs as Jimmy Wood goes into upon slightest provocation down at the Villa. He is surely a born leprechaun.

Theodore Radtke, how could I forget Theodore? How could anyone forget Theodore? Keep your Hollywood image, Ted, with your dark glasses and swirl in your black hair. And keep astounding the rest of the world with your detailed statistics on astronomy. We promise to watch for the total eclipse of the sun in 2024. Don't forget your promise to take all of us on your time machine — to the year 208,932. We'll wear the space suits you are designing, but we don't know about those weapons you are planning to take.

No hamburger will ever taste as good as those with two meat patties served in good weather every Friday noon at Marbridge Park. The boys ask many questions; some pat your shoulder and some stroke your arm; many call to you from across the grass, "Hey, Mama."

I doubt seriously if ever again, when I wear my purple hose, a man will call me "that lady with the purple legs."

I doubt seriously also if I ever have as nice a compliment as from Skinny George Marcus, who tells me how nice I look. He's a handsome boy from New York that is very excited about Texas — so much so that he eats very little. The staff must monitor his meals. By now, thoughts of the above men, with gentle hearts of boys, make me cry.

I am sorry I didn't get to be better friends with Mrs. (Mama) B. She would cry with me, as she does with everyone. But, then she is the old softie when it comes to her Jim — or any of her other "Honeys."

At my only personal interview with Mama B, she was crying when discussing some past times of her life. A staffer opened the door. "Hello, Mrs. B — what's going on?"

She answered, wiping her eyes, "I'm crying, of course."

She has slowed down on her Marbridge work in the year 1988, as she is suffering more and more from arthritis, which in no way prevents her from playing bridge, giving parties, going fishing and hunting, reminding Ed of the Marbridge sick list and planning all the meals at the ranch.

Like her husband, she loves traveling. Both are so gregarious that they usually take other couples along on the trips.

Would you believe the photos they bring back? They may snap a few of their traveling companions or some tourist attraction — but, more often than not, just things they see of beauty, especially flowers. They came back from Hawaii with mostly photos of flowers.

Highlight of all trips for Mrs. B was going to the Holy Land — when she cried an ocean of tears while crossing the Sea of Galilee and remembering when she sang solos in church of "I Walked Where Jesus Walked." She adds that "nothing has touched me so much."

But the second most emotional trip for her was attending the nation's anniversary celebration in New York when all the beautiful antique sailing vessels passed the Statue of Liberty. "Our country is the next thing to my heart," she says.

She is Marbridge's own Pearl Mesta. For certain, her parties are lovely, whether informal or very formal. For the latter, she sends engraved invitations, of course, and more than likely such names as governors and their wives will be on the invitation list. Since attending church is sometimes difficult (with her arthritis), Mrs. B calls the television her "Bible now." She has her own charities; and when she spends money on a party, she soon sits at her desk and writes out a check in the same amount for a special mission somewhere.

"Seems like we keep going," she smiles, impeccably groomed and beautifully dressed. "God gives us the strength, Honey," she says.

There she sits — the picture of a "Southern matriarch" — which she is. Who else would insist on chicken-and-dumplings on Sundays, with fresh green beans?

Her list of friends is lengthy, but they all are remembered by her on their birthdays. "This is sort of my hobby."

Daily she telephones to Mary Leming at the ranch office to stay in touch, check menus she planned and offer advice. She is that "great woman behind the great man." She has been a part of every move of the Marbridge Foundation.

And I shall miss Mr. B, the unmistakable and undisputed Captain of This Ship of Mended Lives. There may be some who do not like Mr. B, although I could not imagine who or why. Through the years of fighting for a burgeoning domain such as the Marbridge Plan, he is bound to have stepped on toes. Regardless, I doubt there is a single person who does not sincerely respect this singularly determined man. It is only human nature to admire a person who accomplishes a "first" of anything, and who sets a goal — and reaches it — under seemingly insurmountable odds. That is Marbridge's Mr. B.

He fought all the way. He fought with optimism and confidence. He won. He has proved that the Marbridge Plan works.

Just for the record, these are some of the plaques on the walls of the Marbridge Board room:

> "Presented to J. E. Bridges in appreciation for faithful service as a member of the Board of Trustees, Mental Health/Mental Retardation Center Austin-Travis County on the occasion of retirement from the Board. April 1, 1970."

> (to J. E. Bridges) "Board of Directors, Austin Evaluation Center designated as 'Friend of the Center' for support and interest with their goals. April 16, 1975."

"The Retail Furniture Association of Texas lifetime member (for outstanding service). July 7, 1968."

"Sublime degree of a Master Mason, Hill City Lodge #456. May 21, 1963."

"Certificate of Appreciation. The Texas Association for Retarded Children." (recognition award and an award making him a lifetime member) 1970.

"The State of Texas acknowledges with sincere gratitude immeasurable contribution of J. Ed Bridges on behalf of the mentally retarded citizens of our state. (Governor) John Connally. July 1, 1966."

(plaque featuring a gavel) "President of Texas Association Retarded Children. 1956–1958."

"Award of Recognition to Mr. and Mrs. J. Ed Bridges in recognition of their Christian service through their life's work with the mentally retarded. First Baptist Church on the 25th anniversary of Marbridge Foundation. 1978."

"Counseling and Pastoral Care Center of Austin (to Ed Bridges) as Outstanding Citizen of our community who has contributed greatly to the quality of life in our city. 1987."

"Pastor William E. Denham, Jr. of the First Baptist Church honors Mr. and Mrs. J. Ed Bridges who in midst of adversity discovered a deeper commitment to Christ and a wider ministry to persons than otherwise would have been possible. The establishment of Marbridge Ranch and all its significant facets is a tribute to the vision, courage and dedication of these two wonderful Christian people. 1970."

(to) "Ed Bridges in appreciation for continued help to the Manchaca Volunteer Fire Department."

"Presented to Ed Bridges for his services as Chairman Austin-Travis County Mental Health/Mental Retardation Center Board of Trusties. 1968."

"Texas Association for Retarded Children. Certificate of Appreciation 1958 to J. Ed Bridges, sixth president, for caring enough to reach out a compassionate heart and hand to lift the lives of the slow, faltering children of Retarded Mental Development to the light of understanding acceptance. That they may more happily grow to their fullest capacity unhampered by lack of support. Inasmuch as ye

> have done it unto one of the least of these my brethren, ye have done it unto me. — Matt. 25:40."
>
> "Council For Exceptional Children Lone Star Chapter 101 Recognition Award presented to J. E. (Ed) Bridges in appreciation for 20 years meritorious service to handicapped children and youths. 1971."
>
> "Award of Merit" to Ed Bridges who was selected by the membership of Dist. Number 8 on the 12th day of Feb., 1958, as their nominee for the outstanding State Retail Furniture Award Winner Contest in recognition of superior qualities and outstanding achievement in the following areas: high ethical standards in advertising, honest and fair dealing with competitors, devoted service to industry through participating in association activities, good reputation in dealing with customers, active participation in community and civic activities. Presented by Retail Furniture Association of Texas, Inc."

In addition to these awards which tell in bronze, copper, and gold, the story of Ed Bridges, the walls of the Marbridge Board room hold a framed letter from President Reagan congratulating the Bridges on their fifty-fifty wedding anniversary in 1981; photographs of every board member of the foundation; and a large picture of a flying eagle under which are the words:

"They that wait upon the Lord shall mount up with wings like Eagles. They shall run and not be weary. They shall walk and not faint." *Isaiah* 40:31."

I learned the story of the latter painting. I thought perhaps it had been purchased at a high price by some friend of the foundation or by Mr. B.

It was painted by Mrs. Ivy Hunt, a former active member of the Oak Leaves, who this year went "inactive." Not only that, but she painted fourteen other wildlife portraits, at the request of Mr. B who placed them in homes of Mabee Village. The Bible quotation for the eagle in the board room was (gracefully) lettered by Mr. B's secretary, Mary Gail.

In this board room are the formal and official wall hangings. You should see the walls in Mr. B's office! First, as you step through his door, there is a mat, saying: "We interrupt this marriage to bring you hunting season!" Beside the door is a package of dog food to take to his home.

Almost ever space on the wall is filled with photos of the Bridges family, Marbridge Ranch and religious and humorous plaques — and, of course, hunting and fishing pictures and photos of animals.

There is a map of the world, a deep frame containing an antique pocket watch with a hand-plaited "chain" of leather, a picture of Mr. B and former Texas Governor Price Daniel signing a proclamation, a poster saying "I finally got it all together but I forgot where I put it."

In one corner is a golf bag stuffed with clubs. New and old balls are in various boxes on the floor. Nearby is a collection of baseball caps. A red one says: "Let a smile be your umbrella and your ass will get soaking wet." Also on the floor are trays of letters, briefcases and boxes containing things probably only Mr. B can identify.

Mary Gail, spreads her arms and says, "This is Mr. B! I don't clean up because he doesn't consider this as clutter." Mr. B is very proud of the prominently displayed painting of the first Marbridge ranch house behind his desk.

On the credenza is his telephone and calculator, a framed newspaper cartoon strip about a dog, and other stuff, all important. He has some easy chairs, a couch, a TV and stereo.

On the large half-circle desk are more of everything listed above. There also are items like a small rock imprinted with "God's help is only a prayer away!"; and a tiny basket with a man's head in it and a note, "Don't ask me, I'm a basket case"; plus crackers, assortment of pens and clips, more pictures, lots of folders, letters and notes.

Mary Gail picks up a little inspirational booklet written by Norman Vincent Peale. "He sends off for books like these — and gives them away, mostly to the staff." A wall of bookshelves bring more of Mr. B's delights: a bumper sticker that says "Animals are kind to dumb people"; pictures of hunting and fishing camps; animal statuettes and crazy sculpture.

"Look at his chair," laughs Mary Gail. Nobody sits in it but him! Nobody!

Oh, yes, one day Bubba slipped in the side door, and they found him sitting in Mr. B's chair, a-grinning. He's one of Marbridge's fascinating Downs Syndrome children, age forty-two. Most of the Downs Syndrome men are full of fun.

One arm of the black leather chair is ripped. Don't bother it; this is Mr. B's chair! Mary Gail says, "Yes, this is his office, and I protect it!"

One additional detail on the president's office: behind his desk is a color photo portrait of a very handsome, well dressed businessman. A

Nature study on Bear Creek trail. From left, Coach Tex Coulter, Gregg Long, Richard Buckle, and Mike Pennington.

little plaque on it says, "Richard Binion, a Marbridge Ex." A trace on this reveals that Richard was at Marbridge for four years, was habilitated and sent back to Indiana where he is working as a managing executive at his family store.

In words of Mr. B explaining the history of his Marbridge dream, he stated, "Somebody had to do it. A need became our Plan." Further he says, "It's been a full life. I needed challenges, and always felt I wanted to do something, and then something else."

"I think I have had more peaks than most men. We will continue and be thankful to God for what he can do."

This writer will miss Mr. B and the magic he has created in the lives of Marbridge men and women.

I may never put my heart and soul into any other books I write. Whoever said that memories are painful was right.

And I hate goodbyes. How can I say goodbye to Tom Beatty, who doesn't listen anyway and asks so many questions so fast that you cannot really get to answer any of them. But he's sweet. How can I say goodbye to Jody who declares "I am a PR man and will help you as much as I can." Then adds, "except I don't get paid for it . . . but I'll do it for Marbridge."

And what about Brian Higgins, who was so excited being able to wear the "joke" dark glasses I wore to lunch one day to make the men laugh. I promised to get you a pair, Brian, and I will.

I'll be sorry not to see the tall and gentle Dale Brinkman, one of the old-timers at Marbridge. He dresses neat and businesslike and speaks so politely with his genuine smile.

Not ever again will I see the smiling Jeff Dickerson or Joe Head quietly coming down the hall with a lunch tray for me when I ate in my office.

I can't believe that I would ever find another place in the world like Marbridge — where these lovable men, with hearts of children, were so proud of their duties and were so pleased to help me.

One morning when the sun sneaked up from behind the horizon reminding me to get up and get going, and as the birds chirped, one by one, I thought how much like a piece of leftover pizza I felt.

It would be the usual long drive — through harassing traffic — to get to the ranch. Reluctantly, I performed the duties of dressing, coffee-ing and starting the long trip. Frankly, I was in a bad mood.

I rounded one of the last curves on the highway and passed the entrance to Mabee Village — and there on a small hill were several of the men, re-whitewashing the carefully stacked rocks that read, *Marbridge.* They had lasted two decades. They will probably be there forever, like Marbridge.

When I drove through the two entrances and slowed down to ten miles per hour, as the sign ordered, I waved to a couple of the men already mowing and trimming the lawns. I thought how much they loved people. I parked in front of the administration building and gathered my papers.

Someone opened my door — and there they were: about five or six smiling Marbridge men. Several shook my hand; all were saying "good morning" and trying to tell me, at the same time, what they were going to do that day. Both Mrs. B's words and Mary Gail's words were on my tongue: "They are all so cute."

"When are you going to finish the book?"

"How much will it cost?"

"How many pages are there?"

"I think my daddy will want one, and my sister too."

"Let's have a book party in the Chapel of Love — it's so elegant!

During the day in my rounds on the campus, I heard these questions and many others. Some I had heard before a number of times.

It was late in the evening when I started home — again through traffic — but would you believe, I suddenly caught myself humming. I actually felt good after a day's work.

I smiled as the words of Pfluger at the Villa echoed: "They keep us cheered up. And they cheer up the visitors, too!"

I shall miss the Marbridge staff:

Ralph Pfluger, with his dry sense of humor; Gary Noonan, so casual with the men while teaching them a needed skill, medical administrator Gary Borchert who pinch-hitted for a cook one day and made the best corn bread I have ever tasted; administrator Shirley Williams, "mama" to the Senior Dorm, who finds them waiting for her to arrive at 7:00 A.M. every morning; Betty Douglas, administrator at Winters Dorm, who lovingly calls her men "a bunch of rowdies"; administrator Wyatt Atkins, head held high, rushing along to do a multitude of things, several men faithfully following along; Benny Howard, Mabee Village administrator, who says he comes over from Mabee, where "everyone works," to watch the ranch folks "drinking coffee" — he's terribly possessive of his Mabee Village.

I shall miss John Perry, bookkeeper, who takes everything with the proverbial "grain of salt"; and Bob Williamson, who has a pleasant way of getting the best work out of everyone. No wonder he is in line to succeed Mr. B!

I won't be hearing Bob say: "Mary, I'm going to hit the dorms!" (Meaning he's going to make his twice-daily check on staff, men, and activities). I know that Bubba at Winters Dorm will be waiting for him because Bubba loves him so much.

Wonder who will move into my office-spot at the ranch? Whoever it is will hear Coach Tex Coulter passing by the door saying, "Hey!" This former All American West Point tackle and star of the New York Giants line has a powerful frame that fills the hall. The frame is clothed in jeans, a T-shirt and that ol' familiar red cap.

The cap is as much his trademark as a Stetson is Dr. Peck's.

Everyone is busy at the ranch, not the least of which is Chris Winslow, who has worked so hard to build the tremendous greenhouse business. But Chris takes time to find a chair for Bobby, who is somewhat crippled and won't admit it, before Chris assigns him the job of washing the onions. This is an important job!

I think I may miss Dr. John Peck most of all. He is the kind, but firm gentleman officing next to my temporary spot, whose job it is to counsel with residents or other staffers. He's the professional psychologist and former university special education teacher who has his feet firmly on the ground and his heart in the roots of humanity. He fits well the Marbridge mold.

Dr. Peck was the unofficial editor of this book.

No, I will miss most of all the men of Marbridge. I just heard Bubba telling Mary Gail that he was going to be taken for a blood test, "and then I'm going to get married."

As I drive down the road toward the gates, the chimes high on top of the Chapel of Love are playing the old hymn my father loved so much: "How Great Thou Art."

Becker is out walking with that strange rocking motion — walking forever in his own world. I pass the field of dandelions which look happy. In the other field the tractor's making a lot of noise. Driving it is either talkative and charming Richard Critz or equally charming and, oh, so polite Doug Payne.

I pass the last columned gate and take a left.

Soon I will pass the proud entrance to Mabee Village. I won't look. It's too much, thinking of those men and women working so hard there to prove themselves wage-earning, tax-paying citizens. They are doing great, Benny and Judy.

Goodbye, Mary Gail, with the sunny disposition.

Goodbye, Mark. Take care of the yellow roses.

Goodbye, Jim. You who are the heart of it all.

Goodbye, Guys. I didn't mind you calling me "Mama." (I liked it.)

Goodbye, Dr. Peck.

Goodbye, Mr. B.

We close this book on the first thirty-five years of the Marbridge Foundation, Inc. and open our hearts to new reflections on life, and to happiness for every single person, including all the Jims of this ol' world.

Epilogue

This treatise was written by Mary Mae Hartley, who thanks you from the bottom of her heart for buying it and reading it. All proceeds from the book go to Marbridge Foundation.

She also sincerely hopes that each of you may find the special hope, peace and love that she saw at Marbridge Ranch, where the staple crop is men and where God and Marbridge hold hands in a solemn pact: that the grass and the men will grow healthy and happy forever.

After a proofreader of this book completed her editing, she sat back in the chair and said, "It almost makes you want to be retarded!"

— and go to Marbridge Ranch.

Appendix

GOD'S SPECIAL CHILDREN AND THEIR MOTHERS

(The following is an Erma Bombeck column reprinted from the Field Newspaper Syndicate, May 11, 1980.)

Most women become mothers by accident, some by choice, a few by social pressures and a couple by habit.

This year, nearly 100,000 women will become mothers of handicapped children. Did you ever wonder how mothers of handicapped children are chosen?

Somehow I visualize God hovering over earth selecting His instruments for propagation with great care and deliberation. As He observes, He instructs His angels to make notes in a giant ledger.

"Armstrong, Beth, son, Patron saint, Matthew. "Forrest, Marjorie, daughter, patron saint, Cecelia.

Finally, He passes a name to an angel and smiles, "Give her a handicapped child."

The angel is curious. "Why this one, God? She's so happy."

"Exactly," smiles God. "Could I give a handicapped child a mother who does not know laughter? That would be cruel."

"But has she patience?" asks the angel.

"I don't want her to have too much patience or she will drown in a sea of self-pity and despair. Once the shock and resentment wears off, she'll handle it.

"I watched her today. She has that feeling of self and independence that is so rare and so necessary in a mother. You see, the child I'm going to give her has his own world. She has to make it live in her world and that's not going to be easy."

"But, Lord, I don't think she even believes in you."

God smiles. "No matter. I can fix that. This one is perfect. She has just enough selfishness."

The angel gasps, "Selfishness? Is that a Virtue?"

God nods. "If she can't separate herself from the child occasionally, she'll never survive. Yes, here is a woman whom I will bless with a child less than perfect. She doesn't realize it yet, but she is to be envied. She will never take for granted a 'spoken word.' She will never consider a 'step' ordinary. When her child says 'Mama' for the first time she will be present at a miracle and know it! When she describes a tree or a sunset to her blind child, she will see it as few people ever see my creations.

"I will permit her to see clearly the things I see . . . ignorance, cruelty, prejudice . . . and allow her to rise above them. She will never be alone. I will be at her side every minute of every day of her life because she is doing my work as surely as she is here by my side."

"And what about her patron saint?" asks the angel, his pen poised in mid-air.

God smiles. "A mirror will suffice."

THE PENDULUM SWINGS

By J. Ed Bridges, President, Marbridge Foundation, Inc.

In recent years there has developed a revolution on the part of parents, judges and advocate groups demanding more freedom for the mentally retarded, more independent living and more normalization in the living patterns of the MR's. Many people would go so far as to close down all state facilities for the mentally retarded and mentally ill. Federal and state programs, however, such as the Department of Mental Health and Mental Retardation, health department, Human Resources Department, federal judges and some unthinking parent groups want all MR's placed in communities in homes of a maximum of six residents and separated so they would be miles apart.

Hurrah and congratulations, for there needed to be drastic changes in the way some private, as well as some state programs were run.

One thinks of the pendulum as it swings in the course of history . . . There is a medium, sane straight-up position of the pendulum at twelve. For too long it had been tragically too far to the left in the history of social work and mental retardation — locked rooms for the mentally retarded in institutions, poor housing, unwholesome and far too little food, or families keeping their mentally handicapped sitting in seclusion at home behind locked doors, becoming more and more ashamed of them —.

It is true that all of this needed correction since as many MR's as possible needed to be de-institutionalized and put into the least restrictive environment.

Marbridge Foundation has been working at this since its inception and has succeeded in placing hundreds in gainful, self-supporting environments living in their own apartments and enjoying the good life in a free society.

So we saw in earlier times the pendulum going far to the left — too, too, far. Now we are seeing the above-mentioned state departments, judges, federal regulators and private programs like Marbridge moving the pendulum past the 12:00 and over to the right into the sunlight of love and compassion.

It is good to consider that in so many instances the pendulum swings to extremes and can go too far another way. In moving to the right, it is perhaps wise to consider that maybe federal judges are creating laws, rather than reflecting the intent of Congress in passing the laws and are interpreting the constitution too liberally. It might also be good to remember that in creating rules and regulations for control of all mentally handicapped, a few of these controls are impractical and a few of them are unnecessary.

As an example, federal and state mental health and mental retardation and other agencies have set up a rule that only six MR's may be housed in one

Ed Bridges presents a recognition award to Dale Brinkman, left, who has been a resident of the ranch for over thirty years. Each man with over ten years at Marbridge receives a similar certificate.

group home and these houses must be three miles apart for the state and federal to pay any money for residents' upkeep. I ask any thinking person what their reaction is to such an unreasonable ruling? This rule alone is costing the state of Texas and the federal government millions of dollars. What is the difference between six residents in a home or eight or even ten if they are properly managed? What does it matter if the homes are three miles apart or one mile or even a half mile?

A few rules like this, and there are a few more just as unreasonable, are causing taxpayers too much money and are perhaps helping to keep the State Mental Health and Mental Retardation Department short of funds.

Reforms that were much needed are shaping up well, it is true. Consideration must be given, however, that the pendulum not swing too far to the right —. The decisions and regulations of unreasonable judges could do this — Let the pendulum be well balanced.

THE PARENTS' VIEW

"When you give parents a cause, there is no stopping them."

Both Mr. B and Mama B believe the above statement, and have seen it "in action" many a time as the Marbridge Plan rolled along to success.

"We always keep good communication with the parents or guardians," says Mr. B. "We operate a three-way plan: staff, parents, residents."

This is how, and why Marbridge continues offering top quality service in its field. This is how weekly letter-writing began, and why a regular bulletin to parents is sent. Every man, whether he writes it himself or not, sends a weekly communication home. Marbridge welcomes parents at appropriate times, all special programs and most parties. Parents are special. Both Mr. B and Mama B can empathize entirely with the parents or guardians.

"I remember well the sadness and emotion we all had in dealing with other parents. They would leave their son and drive away crying. Of course, Marge would cry with them — always. Yet all of us knew this was the best thing to do."

Both Marge and Ed could see again all those times they had to leave Jim.

Ed shakes his head. "It was a scene, over and over!"

But the parents have confidence in Marbridge Ranch. They realize that the founders and operators have a son there also and that they will run the program to benefit Jim and all the others, the best way possible. This instills needed support from the parents. The Bridges also know that a facility like Marbridge has to be run by a qualified staff — not absent parents.

"We have to have certain rules," explains Ed. "You cannot direct a son (or daughter) from his parent's home. It's unfair to all of them."

From the parents' view, W. L. Todd, a current board member of Marbridge Foundation, has this to say:

"After several years of investigating different schools and programs for the retarded, Virginia and I decided to send our son Warren to Marbridge.

"The Ranch is a lively place with the activities geared to the development of the men in residence. The atmosphere is challenging but low key. There is an extensive program of activities, such as bowling, swimming, music, town trips, attendance at football games and periodic trips to Rockport, Texas, and Ruidoso, New Mexico. Under this program we feel that Warren has developed tremendously.

"Since I have been privileged to serve on the board of directors, I have been able to observe first-hand the sincere dedication of the staff, and the caring warmth of the houseparents. The success of Marbridge Ranch is due to Marge and Ed Bridges who have spent the last thirty-five years making their dream come true — and it has."

Mr. and Mrs. Bill Kirk say the same thing. They heard the Bridges speak during the Foundation's early years. The Kirks said they had been told that Bud would be a "pot-bellied, sit-in-the-corner nothing who wouldn't live past the age of 16."

They were very despondent, but after they heard Mr. Bridges talk about his facility, they enrolled their teen-ager. Bud is now a healthy, sunny-spirited, almost fifty-year-old resident in the senior dorm.

Over the years the Kirks helped take Marbridge men on trips to the

Mama Marge Bridges, age eighty. In the early years of Marbridge Ranch she used to take the homesick men in her car and drive them around, consoling them and trying to make them feel happier and more at home at the facility.

beach and mountains. When they retired, they moved to a home in San Leanna, not far from the ranch. Soon Mr. Kirk began to go with a weekly bowling group for the men and for years he has gone with them. Mrs. Kirk has always been an active member of the women's volunteer group.

The Kirks have supported Marbridge financially in a very generous way in everything that they have been asked to help with. Mrs. Kirk approached Mrs. B about the idea of a volunteer group, and together they organized a group that later became the prestigous Marbridge Oak Leaves. The Kirks are two of Marbridge's best volunteers and support Marbridge in every way.

And Mr. Kirk says, ". . . there wouldn't be any Marbridge up there without them (the Bridges). There wouldn't be any buildings or anyone to raise money. He's a super salesman . . ."

Another board member and longtime supporter, Gregg Ring, whose two sons, Brian and Randy are ranch residents, put the worth of Marbridge to his family a bit differently. Mr. Ring said that perhaps the most important service that Marbridge provides is what it gives to the families back home. His two sons were the oldest of seven children: the other five are normal.

Mr. Ring said, like so many others, it was devastating to him and his wife years ago to leave teen-age Randy at the ranch and drive back to Houston without him. He was the first son to attend Marbridge. Everyone cried, and "it was a fight to keep him there," said Ring. "When he was home he didn't want to go back, but, of course, we knew it was best and now when he returns he is happy."

Mr. Ring stressed the service Marbridge gives to parents and the other children at home.

"In giving to Marbridge you're helping normal children. Because parents will give to the ones who need it the most, with a retarded child at home, it is the normal ones that most often are left out."

With two retarded children at home, the Rings never were able to do anything they wanted for themselves and seldom for the other five children. He and his wife were not equipped to handle Randy, who is now in the retirement Villa, and Brian, in Senior Dorm. The two sons have entirely different mental handicaps. They are only eighteen months apart in age.

Mr. Ring said they did not really know the two were mentally handicapped until they entered elementary school, and principals sent them home with the terrible message, so familiar to similar parents, that they did not "fit into the school program."

The Rings heard about the Marbridge Plan in Houston, investigated and liked the atmosphere and proposed program.

In addition to many donations to the Foundation, Mr. Ring opened a branch of his large manufacturing company, the Randolph Company, across the road from the ranch. It was done specifically to give jobs to men trained at Marbridge. Most of the time the Randolph Austin Company employs them as janitors.

Brian Ring is one of the few men on the campus able to drive a truck and run errands. Mainly, he goes for the mail and takes the mail to the post office. He is very dependable.

His father says that "Marbridge has given a home to a lot of people. It has served a good purpose in teaching the retarded how to work."

Marbridge has helped all members of his family, he explained, to live to their fullest happiness: the parents and five normal children in their lives, and Brian and Randy in their special world.

Marbridge really helped our family."

(Editor's Note: The following letter was written by Mrs. Evelyn Marney Phillips, mother of a Senior Dorm resident Mark, and sister to Marbridge incorporator, board member and minister, the late Dr. Carlyle Marney. Mrs. Phillips, who has participated in music presentation and speeches at the ranch, is on the music faculty at the Baptist Theological Seminary in Fort Worth, Texas.)

> The experience is never-failing: I round the curve, and the white stones spelling *Marbridge* rivet my attention as they did the first day I left Mark at Summer camp. Always I re-live, momentarily, that day's sense of separation. Then, as I drive on to the gate, my feeling eases into the realization that *here* despair and pain have been transformed into a victory. This victory began to hap-

> pen as soon as I was able to let go and allow Marbridge to prove they could do more for Mark than I could.
>
> Mark's father died when he was quite young. It was necessary for me to work full time and my greatest problem was to find adequate help in providing for Mark's special needs. I struggled for years with day-care, sitters, special classes in public school and other arrangements. Finally, it was our good fortune to hear of the *Marbridge Plan* and to respond. It offers just what is needed: a place where each person can grow to reach his highest potential; where he can enjoy fine facilities and excellent food; where sports, health care, recreation, as well as religion and cultural development are added to the opportunity to work. Above all, each person is treated with dignity and love by our present staff members — who now stand in a long procession of capable and caring persons, for whom I shall be eternally grateful.

Mr. B said recently that an applicant was enrolled by his parents. Marbridge had received all the paperwork; the new resident arrived at the ranch.

He was not satisfied. All he wanted, said Mr. B, was membership in one of the local country clubs and at least two credit cards. Then he figured he would be perfectly happy and able to live at the ranch!

THE MEN'S VIEWS

"Our cup runneth over . . ."

— *from The Marbridge Experience Quarterly*

(Dr. Peck shares a letter from Robert McLaughlin.)

August 17, 1984

It is a memorable anniversary for Marbridge Ranch! It is Robert McLaughlin's 25th anniversary of the day he arrived at our ranch, sixteen years old, straight off his folks' farm in San Saba, Texas.

So much of this ranch's success has been due to the unwavering dedication of "our men" whose energy and sweat and love have gone into its history! You cannot comprehend the feelings we experienced when Robert walked into our office on the eve of his 25th anniversary and handed us a sealed letter in his own handwriting. Though addressed to me, I wish to share it with the whole world and to say to you THIS IS WHAT THE MARBRIDGE FOUNDATION IS ALL ABOUT!

D.R. Peck
I Come here on aug-17
1959. I was 16 years old
when I Came here. I have
learned alot. I want
to tell you that I want
to make this plade my
home when Earl and auntie
passaway. I want to
live here all of my life
I think that you have
a great place. I think
that you have some
good staff working here
all of the time, I want
to thank all of you
for helping me all of
these years. I know
how lucky I am to Be
here. I can Remember when
we cut cedarpost allday
with a double Bit axe
and Pick corn in the field
with a mule and wagon-
then we would come in
and milk the cows, and
slop the hogs. Robert mc

ALL YOU EVER WANTED TO KNOW ABOUT MENTAL RETARDATION BUT WERE AFRAID TO ASK

"We are a leader in Texas and the nation in proving that mentally handicapped people are responsible citizens . . . who want love and happiness . . . and all they need is a hand on their shoulders."

Important to Ed Bridges during the beginning of the Marbridge Plan was Dr. William G. Wolfe, chairman of the special education department at The University of Texas, who served as chairman of the Marbridge advisory committee. When Dr. Wolfe hired a new professor, Dr. John Peck, he told Ed that Peck would be excellent as a Marbridge counselor. Since that time in 1956, Dr. Peck has been with Marbridge as the only professional consultant on the staff.

Dr. Peck proved to be a great help over the years and has acted as chairman of the admissions committee. As such, he conducted weekly in-house training sessions for the staff. He now serves on the board of directors and continues to act as counselor, although retired from The University of Texas. He has added the professional touch in a practical, down-to-earth manner and proven to be invaluable to the Marbridge organization. Dr. Peck is one of the top mental retardation specialists in the country, and his voice has always been the strongest and loudest against confusing the difference between the mentally disturbed and mental retardates who are capable of being educated.

MENTAL RETARDATION

By John R. Peck, Ph.D, retired professor of Special Education, Consultant and member of the Board, the Marbridge Foundation

In The United States of America, perhaps more than elsewhere, expectation of human competence is built into our very bones and blood streams.

Newcomers to the exclusive circle of World Powers, the American people as a whole, during the last 200 years of their country's phenomenal growth, have come to believe, and have taught their children to believe, that you can achieve almost anything if you try hard enough. Immigrants from Old World shackles as well as their native born successors here have come to believe that if you fix your eyes on the impossible goal and take advantage of the opportunities all about you, your dreams *do* come true!

Amazing as it may seem, this kind of philosophy does bring success and good living to most Americans.

One reason is that our founding fathers had the wisdom to build in the right cornerstones and keystones of government to help common men achieve these kinds of satisfactions for the soul. Not only liberty and justice for all, but a deep sense of devotion to public education and religious freedom became the very fabric of America's panorama for success.

Despite all of this, there have been among our citizens (and among all of the world's peoples) a small persistent minority whose eligibility for achiev-

Dr. John Peck, left, wearing his traditional Stetson, has been professional consultant for the ranch for thirty-three years. Jim Bridges, right, is son of the founders. Center is Delbert Becker.

ing the great dream is elusive or impossible. Do you realize how small *three percent* really is? If you take one hundred of anything and sort out three, you are quite apt to concentrate on the remaining ninety-seven, are you not?

Then what do you do with the three huddled over here in a little clutch of loneliness?

You discard.

Or if the items you sort out are human beings, your compassion may impell you to try to make these three more like the other (normalization) and save them from the scrap heap.

Three percent of the nation's population are born mentally retarded, or they become so during infancy and childhood. The latest (1983) revision of the definition of this population by the prestigious American Association on Mental Retardation founded in 1876, is as follows:

"Mental retardation refers to significantly subaverage general intellectual functioning resulting in or associated with concurrent impairments in adaptive behavior and manifested during the developmental period." *

A crude oversimplification of this definition for the layman might go somewhat as follows:

---

* From *Classification in Mental Retardation,* H. J. Grossman, Editor, American Association on Mental Deficiency, Washington, D.C., 1983, page 11.

He is mentally retarded if he is really below what average people can do at expected milestones in their annual growth "all across the board" — that is, in reasoning, judgment, vocabulary, solving everyday problems, understanding relationships, academic progress, speed of comprehending, recognizing abstractions and other clues to a sound mind for his age, as assessed on standardized measures of intelligence;

And . . .

If accompanying this slow mentality he is significantly limited in adaptive behavior — meaning he is unable to meet standards of maturation, learning, personal independence and/or social responsibility expected for his age level and cultural group;

And . . .

If this below-average ability of his mind is a result of something which occurred during the developmental period, between his conception and about his 18th birthday, the period of his life when his physical brain is still developing.

We can dilute this concept of what mental retardation really is by confusing it with other disabilities we see around us. We see the palsied, the language disabled, the epileptic, the deaf-mute, the blind, the stuttering, the drug addict, the orthopedically limited, the mentally ill — and all too easily we tend to classify them (yes, too many "normal" persons impulsively classify all these unfortunates, perhaps subconsciously) as someone we do not understand and, therefore, they are somehow unacceptable. You help them through charities and taxes, but you don't have to get involved.

All of these disabilities add up to twelve to fifteen percent of America's general population, but in this book we are concentrating on only the three percent who are mentally retarded.

History has been both cruel and benevolent over the centuries to those with mental subnormality. An excellent recent source book on mental retardation from antiquity to modern times is *A History of Mental Retardation* written by Dr. R. C. Scheerenberger and first published in 1983.*

His extensive research describes both the acceptance and the violent non-acceptance of human beings born with and/or developing mental subnormalities. Superstition and fear prevailed more than compassionate care both in the early wandering tribes as well as the mighty civilizations of Greece, Rome, Sparta, and Egypt. It was common to put to death infants born with visible brain damage and convulsive states. Sparta, in particular, where physical strength and perfection were esteemed above all other virtues, was particularly strong on infanticide. Christian influences did help some civilizations to practice restraint, but by no means universally. As centuries progressed

* Sheerenberger, R. C., *A History of Mental Retardation,* Paul H. Brookes Publishing Co., Baltimore, MD 21204, 311 pages, 1983.

governments fluctuated between concern for mental retardates and fear of them, expressed by use of lifetime chains and dungeons.

Early physicians, groping frequently in the dark on comprehending how the neural system governs human behavior, stumbled upon fragments of understanding as they attempted to help the unfortunate. In later centuries it was often the medical profession which took the lead of enlightenment, although the instruments and medications often were only shades away from witchcraft.

There were institutions, although rare, in the Renaissance Period and the Seventeenth and Eighteenth Centuries which arose out of the mire of misunderstanding, where retarded persons and the insane were cared for by a small growing group of professionals. When some of the United States achieved a level of taxation providing care for such non-productive citizens, early state schools for retarded began to emerge copied on the institutionalization movement in Europe. It is important to understand that the philosophy behind institutionalizing retarded adults and children in those early years was to isolate them from society, far away from any community, where they could not be seen or could not do damage to "the good people" of our towns and cities.

The transition of caring for the adult retarded as persons of genuine worth right in the community is a very new experience for residents of our towns and cities today. It is gaining some momentum, but there still needs to be a combination of (1) community services in group homes and vocational placement on the one hand, and (2) institutional care for the most severly retarded, on the other. Nevertheless, Texas and other states are leading the way for acceptance of mildly mentally retarded adults as deserving, dependable, wage-earning citizens in a way it had rarely been envisioned before.

Ed and Marge Bridges were pioneers, especially in Texas, for those from the private sector, who moved away from state-supported programs for adults, they envisioned and chartered the Marbridge Foundation. Here they were able to prove that a ranch-centered training facility for adult male retardates reinforced by sattelite halfway houses in the community for their graduates is a viable and precedent-setting experiment that works.

Though Marbridge is not designed for children, it is well to acknowledge the strides taken in America to bring mentally retarded children out of the wilderness and into the sunlight.

The American scheme for public schooling is one tradition which has been clearly defined but only partially implemented since Pilgrim days: *All children are to attend a public school supported by public funds.*

Human frailty and short-sightedness tarnished this principle for too many years. Child labor laws finally freed boys and girls, including farm children, for schooling; racial prejudice eventually gave way to school integration of children of all races; "the truant officer" made his mark upon ignorant or defiant parents who cared little whether their offsprings got to school; consol-

Picnic in the park at Todd amphitheater on Marbridge Ranch.

idation closed down outlying one-room schoolhouses and fleets of school buses brought the "out back" youngsters to town for more intensive training for the world they lived in; residential schools for blind and deaf children sprang up with state-funded campuses and staffs, and even crippled youngsters began to come in to special centers for learning.

But one less obvious group remained outside the gates of opportunity: the mentally retarded.

There are "so few."

"They can't learn from books."

"But we have state schools where mentally retarded children can be put away."

"Train them for what? They can't do anything."

It was these kinds of responses which Ed and Marge heard in the 40s and 50s as they moved from state to state. To them and to thousands of other frustrated families it was "the old run-around."

One needs to know that no state has ever been able to raise the funds to institutionally house and staff more than five percent of the retarded school children within its borders. If only five percent can be accommodated residentially, where are the other ninety-five percent of our mentally retarded going to school?

The answer in those days: "They are not."

Washington on the Potomac finally heard the cries of this vocally insistent minority. Maybe some seed money from the national treasury could support some experimental programs for retarded pupils in the public schools . . .

. . . But it took a true act of Providence to bring it about. This came in the person of one modest young woman residing in a residential school in Illinois. There was nothing unusual about this young lady. She was a mentally retarded individual from Massachusetts. What *was* unusual was that her father, Joseph P., had been an ambassador to a European nation, and her brother, John, had just been elected to the Office of President of the United States. Her name was Rosemary Kennedy.

Her brother assembled a special President's Panel on Mental Retardation, the first ever, in October of 1961 to whom he addressed the following words:

> Both wisdom and humanity dictate a deep interest in the physically handicapped, the mentally ill, and the mentally retarded. Yet, although we have made considerable progress in the treatment of physical handicaps, although we have attacked on a broad front the problems of mental illness, although we have made great strides in the battle against disease, we as a nation have too long postponed an intensive search for solutions to the problems of the mentally retarded. That failure should be corrected.*

Educators, governors, senators, laymen, parents came alive under this Presidential challenge. The Panel the next year presented President Kennedy with 112 recommendations for action. Delegates from all the states attended the 1963 White House Conference on mental retardation, then went back home and got to work.

Ed Bridges was one of the key workers on the state committees in Texas.

Twenty years later Congress had passed 116 acts or amendments to provide financial backing for the Retardation movement not only in public school Special Education but in areas of employment, health, housing, rights and nutrition. By 1980 an estimated $4 billion per year was being spent on mental retardation and 852,000 mentally retarded children were being served in Special Education!

The thousands of men who have been accepted into the Marbridge program over the thirty-five years of its existence have come from the mild and moderate ranks (educable and trainable), and a limited few from severe (low trainable). The staffing and environment at the Ranch and in the halfway houses are not specialized enough to handle profoundly retarded men who must rely upon life support systems and round-the-clock nursing staff. These latter cases are rare and they need life-support systems to survive.

Nationwide we find that three out of four cases of mental retardation fall into the mild or educable category. This is good news!

---

* John F. Kennedy, from *Charge to the President's Panel on Mental Retardation,* Dr. Leonard Mayo, Chairman, Washington, D.C., Oct. 11, 1961.

It tells us that given the right start in public school special education classes, a job-training experience in a center such as Marbridge Ranch and supportive family and community services later, the educable retarded youth can often move into wage-earning jobs for his adult livelihood, after age twenty-one, or at least be partially self-supporting.

There are hundreds and thousands of jobs in our culture that do not get into the want ads or the headlines but employers depend on steady, appreciative, strong workers at the lower echelons. Our men can often fill those openings more efficiently than a drifting, undependable opportunist from the street, without credentials. Food services and janitorial services are particularly appropriate for retarded adult workers. We also find them jobs in laboratory animal care, freight elevator operation, hospitals, public buildings, sanitation areas, construction, and other such work.

For those men who do not go out into the labor force Marbridge Ranch is particularly made-to-order for lifetime service in ranch operations, horticulture, laundry, dorm maintenance, out-of-door maintenance and construction and many other work stations. Retarded adults do *not* have to sit out the rest of their lives pulled up to the TV and the dining room table. The work ethic has to be instilled, skills mastered, attitudes of service to other people sharpened. Once those lessons are learned retarded adults find promise of self-fulfillment and contentment there at their fingertips with every sunrise!

This is what The Marbridge Plan is all about.

Following is taken from a speech Dr. Peck presented to the Christian Education Conference in Austin for workers with mentally retarded adults.

> . . . We humans are the product of the culture or cultures in which we have been raised. It is no less so for the retarded learner. Your Sunday school pupil in a class for mentally retarded comes with expectations implanted in his childhood and it is not necessary to diverge broadly away from this baseline.
>
> If you omit the singing of hymns because he can't read the hymnal; if you lead all the prayers because his praying is too childish or awkward; if you have him avoid the opened Bible because his reading of the Word is haltingly immature — in short, if you dish out the lesson and expect him to sit and listen every week with no participation, he may wonder why he came. Sunday school, based on his early exposure to Bible stories, to the singing, to reaching God through prayers of the group, can be a rich and rewarding weekly adventure. And he wants his Sunday school to be like other peoples! He wants to be a part of his culture, not apart from it.
>
> . . . I salute those who reach out to God's handicapped children in an attempt to teach the spiritual truths. You will find as you do so, if you employ simplicity and sincerity, that the age of your learners will not matter all that much. The retarded adult, not just a child, is quite accurately one of God's children because he has not, and will not, attain that look of intellectual sophistication known as 'maturity' which the rest of us put on over our confident shoulders. A child can get through holes in a wall which big folks sometimes cannot manage — not

until they have abandoned most of the baggage they've accumulated on the pilgrimage. It's possible that this would also apply to holes in the clouds.

If God made us as we are, and I believe that He did, then it is probably true that God also made mentally retarded persons as they are, 'though the reasons why are not for me to say. Such individuals do have certain advantages over the rest of us, one of which is childlike simplicity. Through the simple truths, through familiar inspiration in music and art, through the Word from the source book of all spiritual knowledge, the retarded learner can touch the very hand of God — and hold tight!

"THE INNOCENT"

She thinks no evil — does no harm.
Her disposition is always calm.
So full of love and kindness, too,
She only sees the good in you.
Anger, lust, they're not real.
Such normal impulses she doesn't feel.
She is innocent. This is true —
Of hate and fear and things we do.
Such perfect trust, so hard to find,
Exemplifies her peace of mind.
With eyes upturned and heart sincere,
Her thoughts may seem quite far from here.
A deeper knowledge, yet not expressed,
Perhaps she's wiser than the rest.
She's sweet and gentle; meek and mild,
She's our lovely Downs Syndrome child.

— From Ann Lander's
Newspaper column,
"The Innocent."

The Foundation's front office is ably managed by secretary Mary Leming, here aided by Jeff Dickerson and Mark Newsom, two Winters Dorm men bringing lunch trays to the office staff.

"Mama B," seated here with her grown up son Jim at a program in the Chapel of Love. Marge Bridges is the first to admit that her tears of happiness are part of the Marbridge scene at these touching occasions.

Shirley Williams, a dorm administrator, explains some of the Marbridge rules to Joe Head and Claudio Ortunio.

Color-bearer for Marbridge Boy Scouts is Tom Raycraft, center, holding the Troop 103 flag. Others representing the troop of forty-plus scouts are, left to right: Nick Mainer, Jimmy Newland, Wesley Jeanes, and John Queen.

Wyatt Atkins is liaison officer and administrator of off-campus activities. Experienced in many areas Wyatt is also the chief officer in dealing with Social Security, an important resource for families of Marbridge residents.

In the television and reading room, four patients at the Villa listen to a funny story read to them by Administrator Ralph Pfluger. Left to right: Tommy Wood, Horace Hanchey, Joe Newman, and Ronnie White.